The Cotton and Textile Industry: Managing Decline

This shortform book presents key peer-reviewed research on industrial history. In selecting and contextualising this volume, the editors address how the field of textile history has evolved.

Themes covered include entrepreneurial, technological and labour history, whilst the book highlights the strategic and social consequences of innovations in the history of this key UK sector.

Of interest to business and economic historians, this shortform book also provides analysis and illustrative case-studies that will be valuable reading across the social sciences.

John F. Wilson is Pro Vice-Chancellor (Business and Law) at Northumbria University at Newcastle. He was the founding editor of the *Journal of Industrial History*.

Steven Toms is Professor of Accounting at the University of Leeds, UK.

Nicholas D. Wong is Vice-Chancellor's Senior Research Fellow at Newcastle Business School, Northumbria University, UK.

Routledge Focus on Industrial History

Series Editors: John F. Wilson, Nicholas D. Wong and Steven Toms

This Shortform series presents key peer-reviewed research originally published in the *Journal of Industrial History*, selected by expert series editors and contextualised by new analysis from each author on how the specific field addressed has evolved.

Of interest to business historians, economic historians and social scientists interested in the development of key industries, the series makes theoretical and conceptual contributions to the field, as well as providing a plethora of empirical, illustrative and detailed case-studies of industrial developments in Britain, the United States and other international settings.

Banking and Finance
Case Studies in the Development of The UK Financial Sector
Edited by John F. Wilson, Nicholas D. Wong and Steven Toms

Management and Industry
Case Studies in UK Industrial History
Edited by John F. Wilson, Nicholas D. Wong and Steven Toms

The Cotton and Textile Industry: Innovation and Maturity
Case Studies in Industrial History
Edited by John F. Wilson, Steven Toms and Nicholas D. Wong

The Cotton and Textile Industry: Managing Decline
Case Studies in Industrial History
Edited by John F. Wilson, Steven Toms and Nicholas D. Wong

For more information about this series, please visit: www.routledge.com/Routledge-Focus-on-Industrial-History/book-series/RFIH

The Cotton and Textile Industry: Managing Decline

Case Studies in Industrial History

Edited by John F. Wilson, Steven Toms and Nicholas D. Wong

LONDON AND NEW YORK

First published 2021
by Routledge
2 Park Square, Milton Park, Abingdon, Oxon OX14 4RN

and by Routledge
52 Vanderbilt Avenue, New York, NY 10017

Routledge is an imprint of the Taylor & Francis Group, an informa business

British Library Cataloguing-in-Publication Data
A catalogue record for this book is available from the British Library

Library of Congress Cataloging-in-Publication Data
Names: Veit Wilson, John H., editor. | Toms, Steven, editor. | Wong, Nicholas D., editor.
Title: The cotton and textile industry : managing decline : case studies in industrial history / edited by John Wilson, Steven Toms, & Nicholas D. Wong.
Description: Milton Park, Abingdon, Oxon ; New York, NY : Routledge, 2021. | Includes bibliographical references and index.
Identifiers: LCCN 2020043272 (print) | LCCN 2020043273 (ebook)
Subjects: LCSH: Cotton textile industry--England--Lancashire--History. | Textile industry--Great Britain--History. | Textile industry--England--History.
Classification: LCC HD9881.7.L2 C66 2021 (print) | LCC HD9881.7.L2 (ebook) | DDC 338.4/767721094276--dc23
LC record available at https://lccn.loc.gov/2020043272
LC ebook record available at https://lccn.loc.gov/2020043273

ISBN: 978-0-367-71588-5 (hbk)
ISBN: 978-1-003-15273-6 (ebk)

Typeset in Times New Roman
by KnowledgeWorks Global Ltd.

Contents

List of Contributors

Sue Bowden has published extensively on the interplay between economic history and economic development, including the crisis and industrial restructuring during the interwar years.

David Higgins is a Professor in the Accounting & Finance Division, Newcastle University Business School, UK. He has published widely on the Lancashire cotton textile industry and, with Steven Toms, edited the volume *British Cotton Textiles: Maturity and Decline*, 2017.

Allan Ormerod had a career as a senior manager in the textile industry spanning seven decades. He is the author of the semi-autobiographical account *Industrial Odyssey: Memoirs of an Engineer and Textile Industrialist from 1936 to 1995* (1996), and numerous articles analysing the determinants of efficient operations in textile manufacturing.

Steven Toms has published extensively on the history of Lancashire textiles. He is the author of *Financing Cotton: British Industrial Growth and Decline, 1780–2000* and, with David Higgins, edited the volume *British Cotton Textiles: Maturity and Decline*.

Introduction

Volume five: contribution and key findings

John F. Wilson, Steven Toms and Nicholas D. Wong

The fifth volume in this series is the second of two that deal with significant issues in the development of the British cotton textile industry. Along with volume 4, the present volume covers the period between the middle of the nineteenth century and the end of the twentieth century. Volume 4 examines the pattern of technological innovation in the mature phase of the industry. It offers some explanation as to why Lancashire entrepreneurs were reluctant to emulate international competitors. The present volume examines strategic responses to the loss of markets and industrial decline during the twentieth century.

The chapters of both volumes collectively constitute a significant contribution to the literature on textile history. Since publication, that literature has advanced in several directions which is worth documenting briefly to set the contributions in this volume in the broader perspective. Unlike other volumes in this series, the current volume, along with volume 4, have a single industry focus, and their chapters are commonly impacted by subsequent research. Instead of individual chapter postscripts therefore, this introduction ends with an overarching postscript on their collective contribution.

In the first chapter, Higgins and Toms investigate the investment decisions of entrepreneurs in the maturity and decline phase of the industry. Before 1914, they directed financial resources into vertically specialised mills centred on mule spinning technology, with profitable consequences. These decisions were rational in economic terms and also consistent with Holden's interpretation of the evolution of the technical alternatives in spinning and weaving, as outlined in volume 4, chapter 2. After 1920, further advances in ring spinning made it much more attractive as an alternative system. However, although entrepreneurs had made vast fortunes in previous booms, including in 1919, capital sunk in existing and now unprofitable mills with declining markets prevented redeployment into new capacity.

The extensive use of debt finance in the boom of 1919 and the expansion of overdraft financing subsequently heightened these restrictions. Control by outside financial stakeholders now restricted options for reinvestment, while investors absorbed any cash that was generated in the form of interest payments and dividends.

The difficult circumstances of cotton textiles in the inter-war period were not closely mirrored in the wool sector. Bowden and Higgins attribute this difference to the absence of excessive speculation and recapitalisations during the short-lived post-war boom that had such a disastrous impact on the cotton industry. Without the endogenous shock of financial speculation and the ensuing paralysis afflicting the cotton industry, wool firms were in a much better position to invest in marketing. They were also less dependent on collective solutions to labour deployment and trade union negotiations. Wool firms, therefore, had greater control over variable cost and greater flexibility in the deployment of labour. As a consequence, they responded much better to the problematic trading conditions of the 1920s and 1930s.

Did the weaknesses that emerged in cotton in the 1920s, therefore, mean that it could not be rescued in the longer run? Allan Ormerod revisits attempts to reorganise the industry after 1945. He argues that the horizontal specialisation that had supported the export function of the industry so well now needed to integrate vertically to orientate more effectively to the domestic market vertically. He, therefore, condemns government re-equipment schemes that offered a lifeline to specialised firms at the expense of firms that were already integrated. Such a sub-optimal outcome resulted from the government bypassing the employers' associations. Successive government initiatives to reduce capacity and rationalise the industry were doomed to failure. The capital investment required to mitigate the labour cost advantages of tariff-free imports could not be made without interim protective measures. Even then, the rate of technical efficiency improvement would not achieve parity in weaving until the 1990s. Meanwhile, the rest of the industry was at risk from the government policy of Commonwealth preference. By the time the productivity revolution of the 1990s created the possibility of integrated advanced textile manufacturing at critical mass, government representatives could no longer see beyond the chimera of cheap labour competition. Instead, textiles were lumped together with clothing, with the consequence that inefficient, labour-intensive garment production was supported for too long, further undermining the possibility of a viable industry.

Taken together, the articles in this volume offer some fascinating counterfactuals of entrepreneurial history. What should entrepreneurs have done, and when should they have done it, and would anything they could have done been sufficient to preserve the industry? Ormerod's paper in particular highlights the social consequences of failure for the dying mill towns of Lancashire. The articles focusing on industry structure and technological choice before 1914 in volume 4 show that vertical integration was a straw man, and that horizontal structure supported both technical innovation and export success. The chapters in the current volume build on these conclusions, demonstrating that the speculations of 1919 created financial barriers to restructuring once vertically integrated ring spinning and automatic weaving in the same plant became a feasible choice. After 1945, the inter-war financial constraint was replaced by government policy mistakes. Over the long run therefore, entrepreneurs were initially rational but successively trapped by their own speculations and then by their elected governments.

The chapters in this volume were published towards the end of two decades of international research centred on firm organisation and entrepreneurship in the Lancashire textile industry. Mass and Lazonick (1990) published an interim summary in their 'state of the debates' article. Their overall conclusions placed Lancashire entrepreneurs in the dock, for their alleged failure to integrate and modernise production. Subsequent research, including the chapters in the present volume and volume 4, challenged this view, as summarised above, stressing technological and financial rationalisations of entrepreneurial behaviour. These interpretations are complemented by coterminous publications that emphasised the role of the region as a source of competitive advantage (Farnie et al., 2000), and of external economies of scale in technological choice (Broadberry and Marrison, 2002; Leunig, 2001).

These contributions represented the last word on Lancashire, and the focus of research shifted internationally. In 2004, Farnie and Jeremy published *The Fibre that Changed the World*, a wide-ranging international perspective on industrial organisation, technology and technology transfer across three continents over four centuries. Their analysis reaffirmed the central role of cotton in industrialisation and economic development, setting the scene for Beckert's (2014) *Empire of Cotton*. His polemical account explains how Liverpool merchants, in particular, operated at the centre of a commanding global network, leveraging institutional support and political influence. Lancashire's decline, therefore, came as countries like India did the same, placing cotton as the centre of nationally organised industrialisation strategies from the second quarter of the twentieth century. None of these accounts belittles the importance of Lancashire, although they do shift the focus from its entrepreneurs. In his 2020 monograph, *Financing Cotton*, Toms switches the focus back to the history of Lancashire businesses. Drawing on the research presented in this volume with a more extensive and integrated dataset and covering the period 1780-2000, he shows how networks of production, marketing and finance first enabled and later restricted Lancashire's sustainability as an industrial district. Only rarely did market conditions provide favourable opportunities for reorganisation along vertical lines, a point which strongly echoes the conclusions of the present volume.

References

Beckert, S. (2014), *Empire of Cotton: A Global History*, New York.

Broadberry, S. and Marrison, A. (2002), 'External economies of scale in the Lancashire cotton industry, 1900–1950', *Economic History Review*, 55, pp. 51–77.

Farnie, D., Nakaoka, T., Jeremy, D., Wilson, J. and Abe, T. (2000), *Region and Strategy in Britain and Japan*, Abingdon.

Farnie, D. and Jeremy, D. (2004), *The Fibre that Changed the World: The Cotton Industry in International Perspective, 1600–1990s*. Oxford.

Leunig, T. (2001), 'New answers to old questions: explaining the slow adoption of ring spinning in Lancashire, 1880-1913', *Journal of Economic History*, 61, pp. 439–466.

Mass, W. and Lazonick, W. (1990), 'The British cotton industry and international competitive advantage: The state of the debates', *Business History*, 32, pp. 9–65.

Toms, S. (2020), *Financing Cotton: British Industrial Growth and Decline, 1780–2000*, Woodbridge.

1 Capital Ownership, Capital Structure, and Capital Markets

Financial Constraints and the Decline of the Lancashire Cotton Textile Industry, 1880–1965*

David Higgins and Steven Toms

I. Introduction

Two issues have dominated the historiography of the Lancashire textile industry in recent decades. These are whether entrepreneurs were rational or not in the light of the constraints they faced and, related to that issue, the causes of the industry's decline.[1] It is not the purpose of this article to review the intricacies of these debates. However, it does seek to comment upon them in the light of new evidence from recent research into the ownership of the industry and its financial performance.[2] Broadly, the argument that arises from these studies is that ownership and governance structures placed financial constraints on decision-makers. Also, the governance structure of the Lancashire cotton textile industry that developed during the nineteenth century had far-reaching consequences for its performance in the twentieth century.

This interpretation has some similarity with others that have contributed to the current state of the debates. For example, it acknowledges the importance of major variations in demand and that in other respects the cotton industry of Lancashire evolved in a path-dependent, incremental, fashion. However, there are several important differences. First, it is not the case that the type of firm structure which evolved in the nineteenth century was inimical to progress and competitiveness in the twentieth century.[3] Indeed, an earlier paper demonstrated that the choice of structure was rational in the light of the profitability of alternatives.[4] Second, the pattern of firm structure did not restrict the range of profitable or feasible technological options available to firms in the twentieth century.[5] Third, although Lazonick was correct to identify the managerial/entrepreneurial split as being at the crux of debate,[6] he did not directly examine the changing impact of governance structures on the evolution of the industry and its consequences for capital structure and business strategy.[7] However, as will be demonstrated in this analysis, governance structures and their associated financial constraints, were the crucial legacies of the nineteenth century.

Collapse in demand in export markets after 1920 and the emergence of excess capacity are well-acknowledged aspects of the problems facing the industry. In addition, as shown below, the new owners of the industry placed demands on cash flow in the form of repayments of loan finance, and other capital, dividend and interest payments. After 1945, these problems were compounded by unhelpful taxation rules. When problems in export markets and over-capacity are combined with these governance-imposed constraints, the interpretation presented here provides new insight into the inability of entrepreneurs to formulate responses to external threats and industry decline. This interpretation is also a variant of the 'early start' thesis that has been used to explain poor competitiveness for the British economy as a whole.[8] Unlike the standard 'early start' thesis, the explanation here is based on the use of capacity created in the nineteenth century and its associated system of finance. These then formed a basis for a series of re-orderings in financial claims as the industry staggered from one crisis to another in the twentieth.[9] Previous studies have recognised the extent of this financial crisis and as a result have concentrated on its most prominent aspect, the intervention of the Bank of England and the formation of the Lancashire Cotton Corporation (hereafter, LCC) during the period 1929–31.[10] The empirical aspect of the present study, which focuses on financing and dividend policies of typical firms (Tables 1, 2 and 3) concentrates on other major firms whose strategies have been neglected to a certain extent, especially in the interwar period. These firms were also selected for comparability through time and whose records were consistently available from comparable sources during the major subperiods of the study.[11]

The remainder of the paper is organised as follows. Section two examines the changes in governance structures and ownership that emerged in the industry during the pre-1914 period and analyses how this led to an over-commitment of financial and physical resources in the industry. Section three evaluates the impact of pre-war governance structures on the ability of entrepreneurs to formulate recovery strategies after the onset of crisis in the 1920s and 1930s. Particular attention is paid to explaining how financial constraints limited the opportunities for increasingly urgent re-equipment. Section four re-examines this relationship in the period from the end of the Second World War to the 1960s, and shows that entrepreneurs remained subject to a similar set of financially induced constraints. Section five reassesses the current state of the debates on Lancashire textiles in light of the preceding discussion.

II. Capital Markets and Governance Before 1914

The boom-slump cycle and continued underlying growth of the industry before 1914 led to important and decisive changes in corporate governance. There were several important aspects to this. First, capital market inefficiency followed directly from the vicissitudes of the trade cycle. Second, market imperfections enabled promotional speculators to engage in systematic wealth transfers. Third, as a consequence of the first two aspects, capital was misallocated in promotional booms and as a result there was always latent excess capacity. Finally, the new owners of the industry shunned corporate saving and instead accumulated wealth privately. Each of these aspects is discussed in more detail below. The discussion relies on evidence from previous studies and also evidence on the financial policies of typical Lancashire companies. Table 1 summarises the dividend and borrowing policies for a sample of these firms.

Table 1 Financial Policies of Lancashire Firms, 1884–1914

Company	*Period*	*Debt/Equity Ratio*[a] *Average for period*	*DPR*[b] *Average for period*
Ashton Brothers	1899–1913	0.86	0.72
Barlow & Jones	1900–1913	1.77	0.73
Elkanah Armitage	1891–1913	0.13	0.70
FCSDA[c]	1899–1913	1.66	0.58
Horrockses[d]	1887–1914	0.85	0.57
Rylands	1884–1913	0.21	0.87
Tootal	1888–1914	1.48	0.49
Sample average		0.99	0.67

Notes
[a] Debt divided by equity where:
Debt is defined as all borrowing falling due in 12 months.
Equity is defined as called up share capital plus reserves.
[b] Divided Pay-out Ratio, calculated as dividends payable divided by profits available for distribution to ordinary shareholders.
[c] Fine Cotton Spinners & Doublers Association
[d] Main constituent firm of the Amalgamated Cotton Mills Trust (ACMT) from 1920.

Sources: Ashton Bros, Barlow and Jones, Elkanah Armitage, Fine Cotton Spinners & Doublers, Rylands, London Guildhall Library, Commercial Reports, Half Yearly Balance Sheets, 1899–1913. Horrockses, Coats Viyella Records (held by the company), Detailed Accounts, Half Yearly Balance Sheets and Profit and Loss Accounts, November 1887 – October 1905 and Lancashire County Record Office, DDHs/53, Balance Sheets, Half Yearly Balance Sheets and Profit and Loss Accounts, October 1905 – April 1914. Tootal, Manchester Central Reference Library, M. 461, Board Minutes, Yearly Balance Sheets and Profit and Loss Accounts, July 1888 –July 1914.

For many modern economists, financial markets can only become more efficient as information flows faster and entry barriers break down.[12] Whether or not Britain had established efficient capital markets before 1914 has been the source of some debate although research into this question is underdeveloped empirically.[13] As far as the capital markets of Lancashire were concerned some clear evidence has recently emerged. This evidence suggests that market efficiency *declined* during the period.[14] Centred on Oldham, the Lancashire stock market began in the early 1870s on the back of a flotation boom of dozens of companies underpinned by the mass participation of the local factory-based population.[15] In the first half of the 1890s, the system met with a crisis. Depressed demand was a function of the loss of the Indian and other Eastern markets, which followed from the depreciation of silver relative to gold on the world market.[16] Capital market efficiency declined following this slump. A survey of annual returns has shown that whilst the typical company of the 1880s had hundreds of transactions in its shares, by the early 1890s the number of transactions fell to only a handful.[17] As the market could not match buyers and sellers, prices could not reflect true values.[18] As we shall see, this had important consequences for the allocation of capital.

Meanwhile, the 1890s slump in values also altered the social ownership of the industry. By the 1900s participation had narrowed and large, wealthy dealers dominated the market.[19] Promotional booms facilitated this process. Such booms, for example in the late 1870s and mid-1880s provided opportunities for promoters to float companies at inflated prices and sell their holdings for large personal profits.[20] This was a rational strategy from their point of view since rising efficient scale, particularly lengthening mule spinning carriages, meant that it paid to build new mills in times of boom rather than extend existing buildings.[21] Meanwhile accumulation of private fortunes meant that next-generation mills could be floated using a narrower range of shareholders.[22] Thus subsequent booms compounded market inefficiency and created new opportunities for systematic wealth transfers.[23] This was especially the case in the pronounced and protracted boom after 1896 that continued with brief interruptions until 1914. Accounting profit rates grew steadily from 1896 onwards and peaked in the boom of 1907.[24] In turn, this prompted an unprecedented mill building boom in the period 1904–8, centred on the Oldham district.[25] By the 1900s, groupings of individually controlled mills became more clearly established.[26] The proprietors of these groups of mills possessed access to financial resources based on reputation and personal contact.[27] As a result they were individually involved in the flotation and directorships of up to a dozen mill companies.[28] These changes created a highly unusual system of governance based on diversified directors and non-diversified shareholders (in the conventional model of Anglo Saxon economies it is the other way round). Hence the rise of powerful directors was not consistent with the rise of managerial capitalism, rather an unusual Lancashire variant of personal capitalism.[29] It was also persistent during the period of decline. The annual returns of these companies in the 1950s revealed similar interlocking directorships and a rump of residual small private shareholders.[30]

There were several important consequences of these changes in ownership. First, the activities of the mill promoters led to the centralisation of capital ownership and the industry increasingly fell under the control of speculative entrepreneurs.[31] As the post 1896 boom developed, their skills at company promotion came to the fore. Profits from existing mills were channelled via the estates of these proprietary capitalists into personally administered flotations or acquisitions of other concerns.[32] They used individual contacts, cross directorships and shareholdings to develop 'empires' of otherwise unintegrated businesses.[33] The late 1890s witnessed the rise of cliques of directors and also the emergence of new combines, such as the Fine Cotton Spinners & Doublers Association.[34] Strategy formulation became the exclusive preserve of these individuals whilst managers became nominee officials at plant level, trusted only with routine. In other words, imperfections in the capital market led to the rise of owner-managed firms that precluded the emergence of professional managerial hierarchies.[35]

A second consequence was that ownership interests were able to impose limits on free cash flow available to managers. As equity holders they demanded high dividends and also used extensive loan finance to fund new flotations. As shown in Table 1, typical companies paid out 67% of their available profits as dividends and the typical debt to equity ratio was close to 1 during this period. Although there is little comparable evidence of calculated dividend pay-out ratios for other industries, it is reasonable to suppose that divestment was higher in Lancashire than elsewhere, since equity capital growth rates were below national averages.[36] Much of the debt to finance new mills came from cash balances in existing mills, and was often used to underpin inter-firm control by cliques of directors.[37] Although these investments occurred without the consent of the residual shareholders,[38] they still reflected the dependence of the industry on local finance, a situation that changed after 1918. This system of finance depended on strong subsequent cash flow to repay loans and also on the willingness of entrepreneurs and promoters to recycle cash from dividends into new flotations.

A further consequence of ownership structure was that the new capacity created by these 'gangs of promoters' destroyed the profit margins of installed capacity and left the industry over-committed in subsequent slumps.[39] The activities of promotional speculators were important because as a result of the 1907 mill building boom, capacity in the industry reached levels that subsequently proved unsustainable. One contemporary estimate was that by 1935, there were still 13.5 million surplus spindles in the industry of which 9.5 million were in the American section and 4 million in the Egyptian section.[40] For 1935, this represents plant utilisation of just 69% in the spinning industry.[41] An alternative way of interpreting this figure is as follows: installed capacity in 1935 was approximately 47 million spindles, but there was only enough demand to keep 33.5 million spindles (installed capacity minus excess capacity) fully employed. Even as early as the 1880s the industry already contained over 40 million spindles.[42] In other words, the capacity that was installed by the promoters in the boom period of 1896–1914 was all potentially surplus in the light of the performance of the industry after 1920. However, if Lancashire's entrepreneurs had *not* responded to the rapid growth of export demand pre-1914 they may have been accused of 'failure'. Any expenditure on plant must be governed by the expectation that the future (but uncertain) returns will outweigh the cost of these assets. Where expectations differ it may be possible to recover these costs by selling the assets to other businessmen. For the first time this drew in significant finance from outside Lancashire. As one authority has suggested,[43] with the development of capital markets capitalists shed their entrepreneurial role and entrepreneurs shed their financing function. The 1919–21 re-flotation boom provides a classic example of this divergence of interests. The over-capacity problem was compounded because corporate growth rates were strongest where private or family control was exercised and weakest where there was dependency on regional stock markets.[44] Yet it was the latter case, best exemplified by Oldham, that led to the greatest expansion of capacity at industry level.

The final important consequence of the industry's ownership structure was for the technological development of the industry. Because the commercial and technical advantages of ring spinning and the automatic loom were not yet established,[45] entrepreneurs ploughed the resources from the pre-1914 booms into specialised establishments using traditional technologies. It was for this reason that whilst there were few advocates of integrated production before 1914, technical issues associated with disintegration came to the fore in the 1920s and 1930s. Thus the critique of specialisation from within the industry, as presented by Lazonick, came from technical experts and managers rather than entrepreneurs.[46] The governance structure inherited from the nineteenth century meant the opinions of mill managers were much constrained by the actions of the directors. During the pre-1914 period, industry ownership and its consequences dominated the issue of technical choice.

III. Financial Paralysis, 1918–1939

After a sharp and very important boom in 1919–21, Lancashire cotton lost ground in several important overseas markets. Particularly significant was the loss of the Indian market and Japanese competition in third markets.[47] These facts are well known. When considered in conjunction with the ownership structure described in the previous section, together with further evidence on financial strategies (Table 2), new insights are offered.

There were several important consequences of this latest twist in the boom-slump cycle that prevented the industry from recovering, as it had been able to do before the war, for example, after 1896. The first consequence was that, to varying degrees, all firms were subject to high fixed charges as a result of the refinancing strategies adopted

Table 2 Financial Policies of Lancashire Firms, 1920–1945

	Debt/Equity Ratio				*DPR*
Company	*1920*	*1930*	*1938*	*1945*	*Average 1920–45*
ACMT	0.65	0.70	0.46	2.12	0.36
Ashton	0.41	0.94	0.91	0.30	0.41
Barlow & Jones	0.85	0.65	0.15	0.19	0.75
Brierfield Mills	0.51	0.39	Nil	Nil	2.54
Crosses & Winkworth	1.35	1.62	4.64	1.22	–0.17
Elkanah Armitage	Nil	Nil	Nil	Nil	2.03
FCSDA	0.92	1.24	1.21	0.88	0.71
Hollins Mill	1.12	1.24	2.47	2.31	1.00
Jackson & Steeple	Nil	Nil	Nil	Nil	1.37
Joshua Hoyle	1.11	2.05	1.98	Nil	0.91
Rylands	0.51	0.57	1.17	0.35	1.27
Tootal Broadhurst	0.44	0.38	0.29	0.31	0.88
Sample Average	0.66	0.82	1.11	0.64	1.00

Notes: Calculations as described in Table 1. Debt equity ratios calculated at each point in time instead of an average for the period.

Sources: *Stock Exchange Official Intelligence*.

during the 1919–20 boom. In 1919 entrepreneurs faced boom conditions even more dramatic than those of 1907. However, unlike previous booms, it was wider margins rather than increases in demand which was instrumental.[48] Also a shortage of equipment and building supplies prevented a new wave of mill construction. These features deterred further investment in physical mill capital that could have only made the subsequent overcapacity problem worse. Instead, firms were re-capitalised such that the capitalisation of the typical company increased by a factor of three. Much of the re-capitalisation was supported by new long-term debt finance.[49] Table 2 provides examples of the typical ratio of debt to equity in 1920. For these firms debt represented two thirds of the value of shareholders assets. Levels of borrowing were lower in 1920 than they had typically been prior to 1914, although they increased to a comparable level, as the crisis of the 1920s and 1930s became more severe (Table 2). Evidence is presented in the discussion below, but it should be stressed at this stage that these valuations were based on dubious assumptions. Some companies, such as Crosses & Winkworth, borrowed to extreme levels in 1919–20 (Table 2). Ignoring the dividend requirements of ordinary shareholders for the moment, these refinancing strategies also had the effect of increasing fixed charges threefold. The annual cost increase represented by fixed interest and depreciation charges was £43,233 for a typical 100,000-spindle mill. On the basis of its average output, that translated into a 2.8d increase in cost per pound on 30s yarns and a 12.2d increase for 100s yarns.[50] To put these figures into context, the average net profit per company even at the height of the 1919 boom was only £14,786. Margins for 32s yarns were 29.88d per pound in 1920, but then fell sharply at first and then steadily to 2.98d by 1931.[51]

Linked to these increases in fixed charges was the second important feature of the boom: a further redistribution of ownership rights.[52] Money capital was invested through the re-capitalisation of existing mills with bonus issues and new loan finance. Like the 1907 boom, these re-flotations were speculative and depended heavily on the reputations and contacts of the entrepreneur.[53] As in all previous booms, new capital was used to finance high dividends to equity shareholders, in particular those promotional capitalists who used stock market quotations as fast exit routes for their own investments.[54] Unlike previous booms, however, money was attracted from syndicates from outside the local area,[55] into what turned out to be a more fundamental mis-allocation of capital. When the boom turned to bust after 1921, as in 1892–5, calls were made on shareholders and exhortations made to lenders.[56] Whilst individuals were bankrupted, businesses survived under new owners. Specifically, the banks became the new owners of the industry in place of speculative capitalists.[57] Their priorities did not follow from any expertise in cotton, and were dictated by the recovery of capital rather than the strategic restructuring of the industry.[58] Even when original entrepreneurs remained, the financial claims of this new group effectively ended local control of a large section of the industry.[59] Again, as with the pre-war business cycle, market efficiency was reduced and the social ownership of capital was redistributed.

The consequences of the revised 1920 ownership structure for the industry were serious and made immediate recovery impossible. The first and most important aspect was that firms could not retrench due to their financial structures and were thus also prevented from pursuing re-equipment based recovery strategies. Retrenchment meant stabilising cash flows through cost cutting or asset disposals.[60] However, neither of these strategies was feasible in post-1920 conditions. Costs had been driven up by higher interest and depreciation charges and they were unalterable without a further re-ordering of the financial claims of equity and loan investors. Asset sales were the least attractive option to loan creditors. The main reason was that realisable values were low. These low values were due to a combination of factors. The collapse in export markets had created over-capacity and hence there was no second hand market. The assets involved were highly specific, especially machinery, and in many cases had reached an old vintage by 1930.[61] New but more expensive technology was available. Book values were therefore well below replacement cost. Thus the only alternative valuation available to financial claim holders was the economic value of the assets in use. As a correspondent wrote, 'the real security for many outstanding loans in our depressed industries is little else but the earning power of the assets pledged' (*Economist*, 1930, p. 394). Such valuations require forecasts of the future earning capacity of the assets. Where realisable values are low, forecasts of the risk adjusted present value of future cash flows do not have to be especially high for a rational decision-maker to support continued investment. Moreover, these forecasts were imbued with a degree of optimism as a result of prior experience of the trade cycle. For example, some recalled the depression of the 1890s and argued that the causes of that depression (high world gold prices) were also part of the present difficulties. As one industry authority, writing in the 1930s, put it, 'though the circumstances and events of that depression (the 1890s) were different in a few respects, the essential causes were practically the same as the causes of the present depression'.[62] These commentators noted that when gold prices fell in the period 1897–1914, the cotton industry had experienced the greatest boom in its history.[63]

A second consequence of the 1920 ownership structure was that the re-distribution of ownership rights during the boom of 1919–20, reduced the competitiveness of those firms that might otherwise have been able to best compete in revised world economic conditions. The newer the assets, the higher the revaluation and the higher the increase in fixed costs. Hence the best-equipped mills of 1920 became the most financially embarrassed by 1930 (*Economist*, 1930, p. 667). As shown in Table 2, Amalgamated Cotton Mills Trust and Crosses & Winkworth became heavily over-borrowed as losses reduced the equity base of these companies still further. In 1919, these were both companies with relatively new assets and in markets not especially vulnerable to overseas competition. By 1930, their share values and market capitalisations had fallen to extreme levels.[64]

A further consequence was that industry leaders resorted to collusive behaviour. This behaviour followed from the restrictions on exit imposed by the revised governance structure. Price fixing schemes were in operation between 1923–4, 1926–7, 1930, and then in every year from 1933.[65] Initially attempts were made to secure industry-wide schemes. However, because these failed to take into account the widely differing experiences of the industry's two major sections, American and Egyptian, they were only short lived.[66]

In addition, financial paralysis prevented Lancashire entrepreneurs from taking advantage of major opportunities offered by technical developments to restore competitiveness through re-equipment. Newer technologies were based on faster throughput and in particular the invention of high speed drafting in 1914. The technical dominance of these new methods was not established until after 1914, and in British conditions investment in new technology only became a potential commercial option in the 1920s and 1930s. Prior to this breakthrough before the First World War productivity in ring and mule spinning increased at approximately equal rates.[67] Only in the spinning of very fine yarns did mule spinning retain its advantages, including the period after 1945.[68] From 1920, high drafting and other improvements in intermediate processes such as doffing and winding provided opportunities to speed up production[69] and offered savings in areas of traditional labour intensity.[70] A survey in 1932 noted three cases of ring spinning mills replacing low draft with high draft spinning, resulting in average improvements in labour productivity of 49.3%.[71] By now industry commentators recognised that 're-equipment was needed on a vast scale'.[72] From 1931, Japanese producers adopted these techniques. This, together with competitive de-valuations of the Yen, explained the loss of Lancashire's traditional Far Eastern markets.[73] Without adequate finance, technological advances were always threats and never opportunities for Lancashire firms.

Finally, because profit streams were unable to cover fixed charges, the financial distress of many large firms had reached extreme levels by 1930, effectively ruling out new strategic investment. However, the tradition of independence of many cotton companies from bank finance[74] meant the financial institutions lacked the managerial expertise required to effect restructuring. In any case, as noted above, individualistic control of mills had long prevented the emergence of professional managerial hierarchies, and remaining businessmen instinctively favoured industry co-operation to closure and rationalisation. As demonstrated earlier, the new financing structure of the industry placed restrictions on free cash flow through high fixed charges. When the dividend requirement was added, managers were left with no available cash to fund re-organisation and re-equipment. Despite the collapse in profits and heavy indebtedness of the 1920s, dividends were slow to adjust to lower levels of average profits.[75] As Table 2 shows, the average dividend pay-out ratio was 84% of available profits. Some companies in the sample, for example, Brierfield and Rylands, paid dividends greater than the available profits whilst another, Crosses & Winkworth, paid dividends notwithstanding aggregate losses.[76] It was these restrictions on cash flow imposed by financial policies and governance structures that informed the response of the industry to its problems, especially the problem of over-capacity. A survey of the industry conducted by John Ryan, managing director of the LCC, estimated the average value of debt per company to be £108,350.[77] At these levels, assuming all the profits earned subsequently were applied to retire debt, the earliest year at which firms would be free of debt would have been 1947.[78] Meanwhile the level of debt remained a significant exit barrier at a time when restructuring became increasingly urgent.[79]

IV. The Impact of Equity and Fiscal Financial Constraints, 1945–60

Lancashire firms did succeed in repaying the excess debt that had dominated their balance sheets in the aftermath of the 1920 reconstructions, notwithstanding the continuing demand for dividends after 1945. Table 3 shows the borrowing levels and dividend policies for a sample of Lancashire firms between 1945–60.

Table 3 Financial Policies of Lancashire Firms, 1948–1960

Company	*Debt/Equity Ratio Average for period*	*DPR Average for period*
ACMT	0.37	0.36
Ashton	0.25	0.29
Barlow & Jones	0.07	0.27
Crosses & Winkworth	0.84	1.07
FCSDA	0.33	0.71
Jackson & Steeple	0.07	0.46
Joshua Hoyle	0.05	0.53
Tootal Broadhurst	0.12	0.36

Notes: Calculations as described in Table 1. For all companies, calculations are based on the period 1948–1960 for average debt to equity ratio and 1949–1960 for DPR.

Sources: Cambridge University Companies Database.

There were two main reasons for their success in repaying debt. One was that there was a minor world recovery in the late 1930s, together with the military demands of the Second World War that guaranteed demand and profitable contracts.[80] The other reason was that many companies took advantage of this breathing space to re-structure their balance sheets again, this time by converting debt to equity as well as cancelling capital that was unrepresented by assets.[81] By 1950, following the sharp post-war boom, the industry had become predominantly equity financed (Table 3). As suggested earlier, the pattern of equity ownership that emerged at the turn of the century was still in place in the 1950s. It now became a new constraint on the recovery of the industry. Also, government taxation policy discriminated against Lancashire companies, further restricting the supply of capital for reinvestment. These two issues are now explored in turn.

The typical investor in the equity of 1950s cotton companies was loyal and not well diversified. Shareholders tended to be old. Alternatively, shares were held in trust where the original investors had died. Either way they did not monitor the activities of the board, whose directors typically controlled significant blocks of shares.[82] The narrow shareholder base was partly a consequence of past patterns of promotional activities, as discussed earlier. At the same time the continued loyalty of some shareholders created a tendency towards thin trading, and thereby prevented others from exiting their investments.[83] The consequence of this ownership structure was that management teams were not motivated to improve the performance of the firm through the normal processes of accountability to shareholders.

Another effect was that shareholders were hungry for dividends.[84] In a thinly traded market they were unable to manufacture cash flow from their investments through selling a portion of their holding. Hence the payment of regular dividends was important even though the fiscal rules in successive budgets in the 1950s penalised such distributions through effective double taxation.[85]

There was a long tradition in the industry of paying out the majority of profit available to shareholders as dividend. As we have seen, this trend was prominent in the pre-1914 period (Table 1), with the result that firms had little free cash flow and managerial hierarchies did not develop at plant level. In the 1920s and 1930s, this haemorrhaging of money capital contrasted with the industry's reluctance, discussed earlier, to reduce its physical capital. As noted above, where profits were made during this period, they were quickly applied to dividends.

Although lower than pre-war levels, high dividend payments continued despite the tax disincentives and the increasing urgency of re-equipment. At the industry level, the profit distributions of Lancashire companies was significantly higher than the average for the economy as a whole during the 1950s. In line with government tax incentives, firms in other industries ploughed back profit and invested in new equipment.[86] Only a small number of Lancashire companies, for example, John Bright, Shiloh Spinners and Smith & Nephew pursued growth strategies in the 1950s. These companies retained more profit, raised additional funds from City investment institutions and increased their asset values. They had larger boards with committed, proactive directors rather than the paralysing governance structures of typical Lancashire companies.[87]

In addition to the governance constraint, there were issues associated with the taxation system that prevented restructuring and re-equipment strategies being followed by Lancashire entrepreneurs. The Chairman of Highams Ltd, provided a useful summary of the problems caused by the taxation system in his 1950 Statement: '... the incidence of the present rate of Income and Profits Tax and their crippling effect on capital development, combined with Purchase Tax are factors which cannot be ignored'.[88] Of course, high rates of tax *per se* will always discourage investment. However, in Lancashire the effect was more perverse than usual due to the asymmetry between tax incentives for investment and the available profit streams against which investment incentive could be offset. Because investment allowances were given as deductions against taxable profits, investment decision-makers would have to be confident of sufficient profits to take advantage of them. For example, a company with profits of £1m per year subject to corporate taxation at

50%, could make investments in new fixed assets of £2m per year and avoid tax altogether. However, marginal expenditure over £2m would not be subject to any tax based incentives.[89] For a company like the LCC, with uncertain pre-tax profits averaging £3.2m between 1949–64 and required capital expenditure in excess of £62m, there was no benefit in this scheme.[90] If the LCC was typical, profit levels for the industry, especially after 1952, were too low relative to the required investment. Unlike companies in other sectors of the economy where re-structuring was not a pre-requisite for growth, Lancashire firms had to bear high rates of tax, but without the compensatory relief of deductions from investment allowances. When combined with the dividend demands of shareholders discussed earlier, it is clear that there were financial constraints on investment behaviour in addition to those documented elsewhere in the previous literature.

V. Discussion and Conclusions

By examining three neglected aspects in the current debate, capital ownership, capital structure, and capital markets, the previous discussion has aimed to offer a new perspective on the decline of the Lancashire textile industry. It is intended that these aspects will be seen as incremental to other causes of decline highlighted elsewhere. Monetary conditions and changes in world demand were of obvious importance but beyond the control of the typical entrepreneur. It is therefore appropriate to concentrate the discussion on entrepreneurial responses to externally driven crises.

Much prior debate has revolved around the definition of the entrepreneur, the scope of and constraints on entrepreneurial activities. Whilst it is possible to agree that constraints existed, the question is which were the most important. Sandberg argued that entrepreneurs operated rationally within the constraints imposed upon them, for example by the structure of the industry. Taking a Schumpeterian view, Lazonick argued that it was up to entrepreneurs to remove these constraints but that they had a problem in Lancashire because *ex ante* horizontal specialisation prevented co-ordinated decision making.[91] There are two problems with this view. First, although not dealt with in the discussion above, there is a presupposition about the desirability of vertical integration.[92] Secondly, if for the moment the desirability of vertical integration is accepted, it is not clear how the *ex ante* horizontal structure of the industry prevented this happening.[93] As the evidence discussed earlier shows, during their careers, some promoters floated over a dozen mills in the booms before 1920.

Through their contacts they were able to raise large amounts of equity finance and additional debt finance through further borrowing. In most cases they built brand new mills rather than extending existing factories. It is difficult to understand why, if the advantages of vertical integration were overwhelming, they did not build integrated plants from scratch. They could have gone further and invested in ring spinning and automatic looms and deployed them in these new factories. Instead, they stuck to mules and power looms in specialised mills. Yet they still demonstrated rational, profit maximising tendencies, as their demand for dividends suggests. Up to 1920, these dividends made them richer, and even more capable of overcoming the constraint of industry structure had this constraint been problematic.

The evidence presented here suggests an alternative view. Ring spinning and automatic weaving established their commercial advantages in the 1920s. Meanwhile a new constraint on investment was dramatically imposed by the financial paralysis of the 1920s and 1930s. This placed constraints on retrenchment and hence reinvestment. In the Lancashire case and in the general case it is sensible to consider the corporate governance structure as the ultimate constraint on the entrepreneur. Financial stakeholders have considerable power to restrict the options available to the entrepreneur.[94] Although 'creative destruction' may be required, for example through the scrapping of surplus capacity, it is within the remit of lenders and equity holders to deny the required freedom of action to corporate decision-makers. It is significant that large-scale vertical integration in the industry occurred only from the mid-1960s, *after* the elimination of so many firms and their capacity as a result of the Cotton Industry (Re-equipment) Act (1959).[95]

From the 1890s especially, managerial power was limited by the governance structures imposed by the mill promoters, notwithstanding the continuing expansion of the industry. The promoters performed an entrepreneurial role that was of its nature unconstrained. After 1920, when ownership was transferred to outside financial stakeholders, genuine restrictions were imposed on action at the corporate level. In this sense the pattern of the industry's development in the nineteenth century adversely affected its development in the twentieth century. It could also be said, paraphrasing an earlier debate[96] that the governance constraint was non-problematic in the nineteenth century but problematic in the twentieth when Lancashire hit the problems of changed world trading conditions. It would be more accurate to argue that the constraint did not exist at all before 1920. As in the general case, in the life cycle of an industry, entrepreneurial power peaks when forecast returns facilitate raising venture finance but before the sale of claims dilutes control. Beyond a certain point the dilution process brings the requirement to satisfy outside stakeholders first and may coincide with the onset of maturity. The same happened in Lancashire. The important difference here, though, was that the effects of transferring financial claims coincided with extraordinary vicissitudes in world trading conditions to produce a crisis and decline of spectacular proportions. Like the industry, the reputation of Lancashire entrepreneurs never recovered.

Notes

* An earlier version of this paper was presented at the Economic History Conference held at Leeds University, 1998. We would like to thank those who commented on the paper, in particular, S. Bowden, S. Broadberry, D. Farnie, F. Geary, A. Marrison, and J. Foreman-Peck. We are also grateful for the constructive comments of an anonymous referee. Any remaining errors are entirely our own.

1. For summaries of these debates see W. Mass, and W. Lazonick, 'The British Cotton Industry and International Competitive Advantage: the state of the debates', *Business History*, XXXII (1990), pp. 9–65 and A. V. Marrison, 'Indian Summer', in M. B. Rose (ed.), *The Lancashire Cotton Industry: A History Since 1700* (Preston, 1996). One authority on the industry has gone so far as to argue that the progress of the product cycle meant it should have become obvious to government and industry leaders in the 1930s that the industry simply was not worth saving. J. Singleton, *Lancashire on the Scrapheap*, Oxford: Oxford University Press (1991), p. 232.
2. For detailed analysis of this evidence, see D. M. Higgins, 'Rings, Mules, and Structural Constraints in the Lancashire Textile Industry, c. 1945-c. 1965', *Economic History Review*, Vol. XLVI (1993), pp. 342–62; D. M. Higgins, 'Re-equipment as a Strategy for Survival in the Lancashire Spinning Industry, *c.* 1945–*c.* 1960', *Textile History*, Vol. 24 (1993), pp. 211–34; J. S. Toms 'Financial Constraints on Economic Growth: Profits, Capital Accumulation, and the Development of the Lancashire Cotton Spinning Industry, 1885–1914', *Accounting Business and Financial History*, Vol. 4 (3) (1994) pp. 364–383; J. S. Toms, The Finance and Growth of the Lancashire Textile Industry, 1870–1914, Unpublished Ph.D. thesis, University of Nottingham (1996); D. M. Higgins and J. S. Toms, 'Firm Structure and Financial Performance, The Lancashire Textile Industry', *Accounting Business and Financial History*, Vol. 7 (1997), pp. 195–232; J. S. Toms, 'Windows of Opportunity in the Textile Industry: The Business Strategies of Lancashire Entrepreneurs 1880–1914', *Business History*, Vol. 40 (1998), pp. 1–25; J. S. Toms, 'Growth, Profits and Technological Choice: The Case of the Lancashire Cotton Textile Industry', *Journal of Industrial History*, Vol. 1 (1) (1998), pp. 35–55; J. S. Toms, 'The Demand for and the Supply of Accounting Information in an Unregulated Market: Examples from the Lancashire Cotton Mills, 1885–1914', *Accounting, Organizations and Society*, Vol. 23 (1998), pp. 217–38; S. Bowden, and

D. Higgins, 'Short Time Working and Price Maintenance: Collusive Tendencies in the Cotton-Spinning Industry, 1919–1939'. *Economic History Review*, 51 (1998), pp. 319–43; S. Bowden and D. M. Higgins, 'Quiet Successes and Loud Failures: The UK Textile Industries in the Interwar Years', *Journal of Industrial History*, Vol. 3 (1) (2000), pp. 91–111; S. J. Procter and J. S. Toms, 'Industrial Relations and Technical Change: Profits, Wages and Costs in the Lancashire Cotton Industry, 1880–1914, *Journal of Industrial History,* Vol. 3 (1) (2000), pp. 54–72; D. M. Higgins and J. S. Toms, 'Public Subsidy and Private Divestment: The Lancashire Cotton Textile Industry', *Business History*, Vol. 42 (1) (2000), pp. 59–84; J. S. Toms, 'The Rise of Modern Accounting and the Fall of the Public Company', *Accounting Organizations and Society* (2000, forthcoming). For preliminary results of further surveys in this area, see D. M. Higgins and J. S. Toms, 'Corporate Borrowing, Financial Distress and Industrial Decline: The Lancashire Cotton Textile Industry, 1918–1931', *University of Nottingham Discussion Papers* (2000); I. Filatotchev and J. S. Toms, 'Corporate Governance, Strategy and Survival in a Declining Industry: A Study of Lancashire Textile Companies', *Birkbeck College Discussion Paper* (2000); J. S. Toms, 'Information Content of Earnings in an Unregulated Market: The Co-operative Cotton Mills of Lancashire, 1880–1900' (unpublished working paper). In view of the preliminary nature of the later citations, where appropriate, relevant evidence from them is also presented in the current paper.

3. The view that the pattern of development in the nineteenth century adversely affected performance in the twentieth is advocated most strongly by Lazonick. See, especially, W. Lazonick, 'Competition, Specialisation, and Industrial Decline', *Journal of Economic History*, Vol. 41 (1981), pp. 31–8; W. Lazonick, 'Industrial Organization and Technological Change: The Decline of the British Cotton Industry', *Business History Review,* Vol. 57 (1983), pp. 195–236.
4. Higgins and Toms, 'Firm Structure and Financial Performance'.
5. Higgins, 'Rings, Mules and Structural Constraints'; G. Saxonhouse, and G. Wright, 'New Evidence on the Stubborn English Mule and the Cotton Industry, 1878–1920', *Economic History Review*, Vol. 37 (1984), pp. 507–19.
6. Lazonick, 'Competition, Specialisation, and Industrial Decline'; Lazonick, 'Industrial Organization and Technological Change; W. Lazonick, 'The Cotton Industry', in B. Elbaum and W. A. Lazonick (eds), *The Decline of the British Economy*, Oxford: Oxford University Press, pp. 39–45.
7. In the ensuing discussion it is accepted that there is a distinction between managers and entrepreneurs. Managers are concerned with the day to day running of the business, whereas entrepreneurs are concerned with strategic issues.
8. For example, S. Pollard, *Britain's Prime and Britain's Decline*, London: Edward Arnold (1990).
9. The central importance of capacity acquired during the nineteenth century and the problems of maladjustment it posed in the twentieth century when demand collapsed, has recently been emphasised for another staple industry, shipbuilding, during the inter-war years. F. Geary,

'The Emergence of Mass Unemployment: Wages and Employment in Shipbuilding between the Wars', *Cambridge Journal of Economics*, Vol. 21 (1997), pp. 303–21.

10. For example J. Bamberg, The Government, the Banks, and the Lancashire Cotton Industry, 1918–1939, Unpublished Ph.D. thesis, University of Cambridge, 1984; J. Bamberg, 'The Rationalization of the British Cotton Industry in the Interwar Years', *Textile History*, Vol. 19 (1) (1988), pp. 83–102; R. S. Sayers, *The Bank of England, 1891–1944*, Cambridge, Cambridge University Press (1976); H. Sjogren, 'Financial Recontruction and Industrial Reorganisation in Differenct Systems: A Comparative View of British and Swedish Institutions during the Inter-War Period', *Business History*, Vol. 40 (1) (1998), pp. 84–105.
11. The principal sources were the Companies Archive at the London Guildhall Library, the *Stock Exchange Official Year-Book* and the Cambridge University Companies Database. To a certain extent, therefore, the evidence and argument presented here only relate to large publicly quoted companies.
12. I. Walter and R. Smith, *Global Capital Markets and Banking*, London, McGraw Hill (1999), pp. 198–200.
13. D. McCloskey, *Knowledge and Persuasion in Economics*, Cambridge: Cambridge University Press (1994), p. 154.
14. Toms, 'The Rise of Modern Accounting and the Fall of the Public Company' and Toms, 'Information Content of Earnings in an Unregulated Market.
15. W. Thomas, The Provincial Stock Exchanges, London: Frank Cass (1973), p. 147.
16. For a discussion of the political economy of silver depreciation, A. Howe, 'Bimetallism, *c.* 1880–1898: A Controversy Re-opened?' *English Historical Review*, Vol. CV, July (1990), pp. 377–91; E. Green, 'Rentiers versus Producers? The Political Economy of the Bimetallic Controversy, *c.* 1880–98', *English Historical Review*, CIII, July (1988), pp. 588–612; E. Green, 'The Bimetallic Controversy: Empiricism Belimed or the Case for the Issues', *English Historical Review*, CV, July (1990), pp. 674–83. An econometric analysis of gold prices and cotton profits shows a strong association, see Toms, The Finance and Growth of the Lancashire Cotton Textile Industry, Ch. 11.
17. Toms, 'The Rise of Modern Accounting and the Fall of the Public Company'.
18. In 1891 the *Oldham Standard* reported that, 'the published list of market prices is not a very reliable guide just now, as they are either nominal or too wide in price to be of practical use' (*Oldham Standard*, 1 August, 1891).
19. As illustrated by an analysis of the share registers of Lancashire companies. For details, see Toms, 'The Rise of Modern Accounting and the Fall of the Public Company'.
20. D. Farnie, *The English Cotton Industry and the World Market*, Oxford: Clarendon Press (1979).
21. G. Wood, 'The Statistics of Wages in the Nineteenth Century Cotton Industry', *Journal of the Royal Statistical Society*, Vol. LXXIII (1910), pp. 585–626; R. Tyson, 'The Cotton Industry', in Aldcroft D. H. (ed.)

The Development of British Industry and Foreign Competition, 1875–1914, London (1968) , p. 123.

22. Toms, 'The Rise of Modern Accounting and the Fall of the Public Company'.
23. *Ibid.*
24. Toms, 'Growth, Profits and Technological Choice', pp. 39 and 44.
25. During the period 1897–1913 installed spindleage increased by 2 per cent per annum in Lancashire but by 2.7 per cent in Oldham (calculated from Robson, R., *The Cotton Industry in Britain*, London: Macmillan, 1957, Tables 2 and 5, pp. 334 and 340; and Farnie, *The English Cotton Industry,* p. 42.) The higher rate in Oldham was a function of the extraordinary boom of the middle years of the 1900s. For details of the mills constructed, see F. Jones, The Cotton Spinning Industry in the Oldham District from 1896–1914. Unpublished MA thesis, University of Manchester, 1959, pp. 221–3.
26. Toms, 'The Supply of and the Demand for Accounting Information' p. 228.
27. R. E. Tyson, Sun Mill: A Study in Democratic Investment, Unpublished MA thesis, University of Manchester, 1962; W. Thomas, *The Provincial Stock Exchanges*; Toms, 'The Supply of and the Demand for Accounting Information', p. 228.
28. For examples of individual entrepreneurs see Toms, 'The Supply of and the Demand for Accounting Information', p. 228; Toms 'The Rise of Modern Accounting'; D. Gurr and J. Hunt, *The Cotton Mills of Oldham*, Oldham, Oldham Leisure Services (1985), pp. 9–10. In the 1873–5 boom alone William Nuttall was involved in the flotation of 12 mills, Thomas, *The Provincial Stock Exchanges*, p. 146. During the period 1899–1914, one firm of accountants floated 12 mills, Jones, The Cotton Spinning Industry, p. 13.
29. Managerial capitalism refers to a managerial hierarchy facing a diversified group of equity investors; personal capitalism refers to owners treating their businesses as personal estates. A. Chandler, *Scale and Scope: The Dynamics of Industrial Capitalism*, Cambridge, Mass.: Belknap Press (1990).
30. Filatotchev and Toms, 'Corporate Governance, Strategy and Survival in a Declining Industry'. This conclusion is based on a survey of the Annual Returns (Form E) of a sample of 29 companies from the period 1950–1965 from the BT31 file at the Public Record Office.
31. Toms, The Finance and Growth of the Lancashire Cotton Textile Industry, pp. 226–31.
32. Toms, 'Financial Constraints on Economic Growth', p. 380; Toms, 'The Finance and Growth of the Lancashire Cotton Textile Industry', pp. 328–9; Toms, 'Windows of Opportunity in the Textile Industry', p. 16.
33. Typically, there were no stock market based acquisitions and mergers in the Oldham district. Instead entrepreneurs preferred to float and build new mills. Toms, The Finance and Growth of the Lancashire Textile Industry, p. 231; Toms, 'The Supply of and Demand for Accounting Information' p. 230.
34. Toms, 'The Demand for and Supply of Accounting Information', pp. 226–231; H. Macrosty, *The Trust Movement in British Industry*, London: Longmans (1907), pp. 124–5.

35. Toms 'Financial Constraints on Economic Growth', p. 380; Toms, The Finance and Growth of the Lancashire Textile Industry, pp. 217–38; Toms, 'Windows of Opportunity in the Textile Industry', p. 10.
36. For further evidence on debt and dividend policies, see Toms, 'Windows of Opportunity in the Textile Industry', pp. 3–9. See Table 1, p. 4 for a comparison between sections of the Lancashire textile industry with national average rates of capital accumulation.
37. Jones, 'The Cotton Spinning Industry', pp. 38 and 88.
38. Tyson, 'Sun Mill', p. 295.
39. Jones, The Cotton Spinning Industry in the Oldham District, p. 3.
40. T. Barlow, 'Surplus capacity in the Lancashire Cotton Industry', *Manchester School*, Vol. 6 (1935), p. 35.
41. Robson, *The Cotton Industry*, Table 8, p. 344.
42. Calculated from Robson, *The Cotton Industry,* Table 5, p. 340.
43. S. Wu, *Production, Entrepreneurship and Profits*, Oxford: Blackwell (1989).
44. Toms, 'Windows of Opportunity in the Textile Industry', p. 3.
45. See, for example, Saxonhouse and Wright, 'New Evidence on the Stubborn English Mule', p. 519. A more recent discussion of the commercial and technological factors which affected the adoption of ring spinning during the inter-war years is contained in Higgins and Toms, 'Firm Structure and Financial Performance', pp. 212–14.
46. Developments in intermediate processing, principally high drafting, doffing and winding, that were developed and available commercially after 1914, gave a decisive advantage to the ring and automatic loom combination by the 1930s. Toms, 'Growth, Profits and Technological Choice'. For examples of technicians' criticisms of industry structure, see Lazonick, 'Industrial Organization and Technological Change'; B. Robinson, 'Business Methods in the Cotton Trade' *Journal of the British Association of Managers of Textile Works,* Vol. IX (1918–9), and F. Holt, 'High Speed Winding and Warping' *Journal of the National Federation of Textile Managers' Associations*, Vol. IX (1929–30), pp. 104–5.
47. A. Burnett-Hurst, 'Lancashire and the Indian market', *Journal of the Royal Statistical Society*, Vol. 95 (1932) pp. 395–454; B. Ellinger and H. Ellinger, 'Japanese competition in the Cotton Trade, *Journal of the Royal Statistical Society*, Vol. 93 (1930), pp. 185–218.
48. *Ibid*., p. 170.
49. Thomas, *The Provincial Stock Exchanges*, pp. 159–60.
50. For example see the calculations in T. Thornley, *Modern Cotton Economics*, London: Scott Greenwood and Son (1923), pp. 187–9.
51. Robson, *The Cotton Industry*, pp. 336 and 338.
52. Thomas, *The Provincial Stock Exchanges*, p. 156.
53. Samuel Firth Mellor and Frank Platt were typical of the entrepreneurs involved. Thomas, *The Provincial Stock Exchanges,* p. 157; Bamberg, The Government, the Banks, and the Lancashire Cotton Industry, p. 6.
54. For example the premature retirement of Frank Platt. Bamberg, 'Sir Frank Platt', in D. Jeremy (ed.), *Dictionary of Business Biography*, London: Butterworths (1984–6); Thomas, *The Provincial Stock Exchanges,* p. 158.
55. Thomas, *The Provincial Stock Exchanges*, p. 157.

56. As in the 1890s, when calls were made on share capital, equity investors responded by withdrawing loan money from other companies. G. Daniels, and J. Jewkes, 'The post-war depression in the Lancashire cotton industry', *Journal of the Royal Statistical Society*, Vol. 91 (1928), pp. 179–80.
57. By 1926 it was claimed, a large section of the industry was 'practically in the hands of the banks'. *Ibid.*, p. 161.
58. Keynes recognised that the need of the banks to secure their original advances with fresh advances reduced the exit of inefficient firms and increased the need for short-time working. J. M. Keynes, 'Industrial reorganisation: cotton', in Moggeridge, D. M. (ed.), *The Collected Writings of John Maynard Keynes*, Vol. 19 (1926), p. 584.
59. *Ibid.*, p. 162.
60. Strategic management theory suggests that firms responding to crisis should follow these strategies as precursors to further action. See for example, J. A. Pearce, and K. D. Robbins, 'Towards Improved Theory and Research on Business Turnaround', *Journal of Management*, Vol. 19 (1993), pp. 613–36; F. Zimmerman, *The Turnaround Experience,* New York: McGraw-Hill (1991).
61. J. Ryan, 'Machinery Replacement in the Cotton Trade', *Economic Journal*, Vol. 40 (December), pp. 568–80.
62. Federation of Master Cotton Spinners' Associations (FMCSA), *Measures for the Revival of the Lancashire Cotton Industry*, Manchester: FMCSA (1936), p. 7.
63. *Economist*, 1930, p. 520; FMCSA, *Measures for the Revival.*
64. *Stock Exchange Official Year Books*, 1930 and 1931.
65. Collusive policies were recognised by Keynes: '(they) are founded on the belief that, if only industries hang on, 'normal' times will return when they may again hope to employ plant and capital on profitable terms'. J. M. Keynes, *Collected Writings*, Vol. XIX, *Activities 1922–1929: The Return to Gold and Industrial Policy* II, 'Industrial Reorganisation: Cotton', p. 579.
66. Bowden and Higgins, 'Short Time Working and Price Maintenance', pp. 330–31.
67. Higgins and Toms, 'Firm Structure and Financial Performance', p. 213.
68. Higgins, 'Rings, Mules, and Structural Constraints'; Higgins, 'Re-equipment as a Strategy for Survival'.
69. H. Catling, *The Spinning Mule*, Newton Abbot: David and Charles (1970), p. 189; Noguera, S., *Theory and Practice of High Drafting*, privately published (1936), pp. 20–3; L. Tippett, *A Portrait of the Lancashire Cotton Industry*, Oxford: Oxford University Press (1969).
70. Procter and Toms, 'Industrial Relations and Technical Change'.
71. Board of Trade, *An Industrial Survey of the Lancashire Area (Excluding Merseyside)*, London: HMSO (1932), p. 135.
72. *Economist*, 1930, p. 394.
73. D. Farnie and T. Abe, 'Japan, Lancashire and the Asian Market for Cotton Manufactures, 1890–1990', in Farnie, D., Nakaoka, T., Jeremy, D., Wilson, J. and Abe, T. (eds), *Region and Strategy in Britain and Japan*, London: Routledge (2000).
74. Toms, 'Windows of Opportunity in the Textile Industry', p. 8.

75. Most companies avoided liquidation and indeed some continued to pay dividends; see the example of the large dividends paid by Lilac Mill in 1925 and 1926, in Thomas, *The Provincial Stock Exchanges*, p. 160.
76. In both cases this amounted to funding dividends by running down reserves, a strategy likely to damage the interests of loan creditors.
77. Bamberg, The Government, the Banks, and the Lancashire Cotton Industry, Appendix 4.1, p. 122. Unfortunately, this data does not give the exact amount of debt owned by each company entering the LCC. It does, however, give a range of the amounts owed to creditors. By taking the mid-point of each range, it is possible to calculate the average indebtedness of the 321 companies surveyed by Ryan and the average indebtedness of companies entering the LCC.
78. Robson, *The Cotton Industry*, Table 4, p. 338. Summing all the profits from 1935 to 1947 yields £109,339. This calculation makes no allowance for trading losses accumulated throughout the 1920s.
79. In this context our interpretation of the industry's twentieth-century performance does have some similarities with those recently advanced by Lorenz. However, while we agree that there was 'excess inertia', we view this as a rational strategy by the industry's businessmen to preserve their physical assets in order to be able to divest money capital as fully as possible, rather than simply as conservatism. E. Lorenz, 'Organisational Inertia and Competitive Decline: The British Cotton, Shipbuilding and Car Industries, 1945–1975', *Industrial and Corporate Change*, Vol. 3 (1994), pp. 387–8.
80. J. Singleton, 'The Decline of the Cotton Industry since 1940' in M. B. Rose (ed.), *The Lancashire Cotton Industry: A History Since 1700*, Preston (1996), pp. 300–1.
81. For example, Barlow and Jones, Crosses and Winkworth, FCDSA and Jackson & Steeple carried out schemes in 1936, 1944, 1942 and 1943 respectively, *Stock Exchange Official Year-Book*.
82. Filatotchev and Toms, 'Corporate Governance, Strategy and Survival in a Declining Industry'. This conclusion is based on a survey of the Annual Returns (Form E) of a sample of 29 companies from the period 1950–1965 from the BT31 file at the Public Record Office.
83. For evidence of capital market inefficiency in this period, see Higgins and Toms, 'Public Subsidy and Private Divestment', p. 72, especially n. 74.
84. *Ibid.*, Figure 1, p. 64.
85. Political and Economic Planning, *Growth in the British Economy*, London (1960), p. 123.
86. Higgins and Toms, 'Public Subsidy and Private Divestment', pp. 66–7.
87. Filatotchev and Toms, 'Corporate Governance, Strategy and Survival in a Declining Industry'. The evidence refers to a sample of 29 firms taken from PRO BT31, 1950–65.
88. Annual Report and Accounts, 1950, Companies House.
89. Higgins and Toms, 'Public Subsidy and Private Divestment', p. 68.
90. Average profits calculated from Cambridge University Companies Database. See also GMRO/LCC, Annual Reports, 1953/4 for details of capital expenditure requirement.
91. L. Sandberg, Lancashire in Decline, Columbus, Ohio (1974); Lazonick, 'Competition, Specialisation, and Industrial Decline'; Lazonick,

'Industrial Organization and Technological Change'; Lazonick, 'The Cotton Industry'.

92. A comparative empirical study has shown that profit signals did not suggest the superiority of vertical integration. Higgins and Toms, 'Firm Structure and Financial Performance'.
93. For an additional perspective on this point, see G. Saxonhouse, and G. Wright, 'Stubborn Mules and Vertical Integration: The Disappearing Constraint', *Economic History Review*, 2nd Ser. Vol. XL(i) (1987), pp. 87–94.
94. V. Barker, and I. Duhaime, 'Strategic Change in the Turnaround Process: Theory and Empirical Evidence', *Strategic Management Journal*, Vol. 18 (1997), pp. 13–38.
95. A number of contemporaries, especially during the inter-war years, were well aware of the vital importance of *first* removing excess capacity. G. C. Allen, *British Industries and their Organisation*, London: Longmans, Green (1959), pp. 239–40; H. Clay, *Report on the Position of the English Cotton Industry*, Confidential Report for Securities Management Trust (1931), p. 83. For Keynes, policies of short-time working and price maintenance merely delayed the introduction of much needed measures to reduce capacity. Keynes, 'Industrial Reorganisation', pp. 590–8.
96. Mass and Lazonick, 'The British Cotton Industry and International Competitive Advantage'.

2 Quiet Successes and Loud Failures

The UK Textile Industries in the Inter-war Years*

Sue Bowden and David Higgins

I.

A literature review might leave the uninitiated with the view that textile industries can be 'lumped' together and treated as a whole during the inter-war period, and that the only interesting sector is that of cotton textiles. Such an impression is grossly misleading; it does not do justice to the woollen textile industry. Indeed, when compared with the cotton textile industry, the woollen industry appears to have been remarkably successful. Wool textiles weathered the depression, continued to perform well in overseas markets, withstood import competition, maintained pre-war output levels and recorded unemployment levels which were markedly less severe than the cotton industry.[1] Yet the story of this success, and still less the explanation, has not been told.[2]

This paper suggests that the literature would benefit from a closer comparative examination of the wool and cotton textile industries. Section II evaluates the export and output performance of the two industries. Particular emphasis is placed upon conduct rather than structural variables to explain the different performances of the two industries. Section III examines the marketing performance, both export and domestic, of the woollen industry. Insights from product cycle theories of trade on the one hand, and Chandlerian marketing methods on the other, are used to explain, respectively, export and domestic sales performance. In Section IV we contrast the ruinous speculation suffered by the cotton industry as a result of the reflotation boom, 1919–1921, with the absence of such excesses in the woollen industry. A major feature of this section is our argument that industries can suffer just as much from endogenous shocks, which have hysteresis effects, as they can from exogenous shocks (such as a collapse in export markets). Labour relations in both industries are discussed in Section V. Unlike the spinning and weaving sections of the cotton industry, the woollen industry devoted much less effort to trying to shore up industry-wide collective bargaining, especially during the 1930s. This gave firms in the woollen industry a much greater degree of flexibility in controlling their labour costs. Section VI draws together some of the principal conclusions which emerge from this paper.

II.

It is not difficult to see why scholars have preferred to devote their attentions to analyses of the cotton rather than the wool textile industries. Prior to the First World War, the export performance of the latter was dwarfed by that of cotton textiles. Although the West Riding woollen industry had risen to prominence initally as an export-led region, it was cotton rather than wool textiles which dominated export markets. Despite the fall-back in 1908, cotton textiles' record was one of high growth and high value. Woollen exports were, by comparison, of low value and demonstrated an all-but-static growth pattern.

It is tempting to conclude that differences between the fortunes of the cotton and wool textile industries during the inter-war years can be accounted for entirely by the differential impact of demand shocks. Both industries experienced substantial demand shocks, but they were far more severe for the cotton industry than they were for the woollen industry (Figure 1). Between 1912 and 1935, exports of cotton manufactures and exports of cotton yarn declined by 71 and 42 per cent respectively. For the woollen industry during the same period, exports of woven tissues and exports of worsted yarn fell by 54 and 24 per cent respectively, while exports of woollen yarn managed a slight increase of 1.6 per cent.

The principal explanation for cotton's precipitous decline was the loss of the Indian market and Japanese competition in third markets. India was the greatest single market for Lancashire's goods. Out of a total British production of about 700m yards of cotton piece goods in 1913, 43 per cent by quantity and 36 per cent by value were exported to India.[3] The inter-war years witnessed a substantial rise in India's own production of cotton manufactures; by the early 1930s Indian production of cotton piece goods and yarn was 34 per cent and 131 per cent greater respectively than her pre-war average.[4]

Cotton's markets collapsed further as a result of the growth of the cotton textile industry in Japan. Aggressive sales policies, substantial

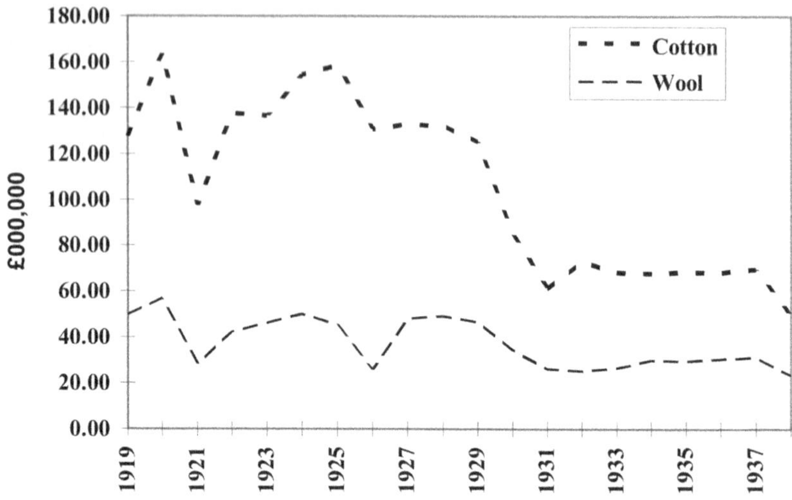

Figure 1 Real Value of Cotton and Wool Exports from the UK, 1919–1938

Source: Mitchell and Deane, Table 8, p. 396.

credit facilities provided by Japanese banks and the higher levels of vertical integration in the textile industry have all been forwarded to explain Japan's success in this period.[5]

Despite the massive dislocation caused by the First World War, woollen exports as a whole (tissues, worsted and woollen yarns) rebounded positively. Indeed, apart from one or two isolated speculative shocks,[6] the export performance of the general woollen industry was strong throughout the 1920s. It is only from the onset of the global depression in the early 1930s, that the woollen exports fell (Figure 2).

Woollen textiles did not face competition in third markets on the scale experienced by cotton textiles. The stagnation in exports was not the result of the success of other export countries in capturing British markets. Any fall-back reflected a continuation of pre-war trends whereby consuming countries increasingly met their own requirements.[7] The net result of this was that world trade in wool goods contracted, but of the diminishing volume of trade, UK manufacturers retained a large and increasing share.[8]

Whereas cotton manufacturers witnessed the collapse of former key markets as India and Japan produced cotton goods, neither country posed any threat to the woollen industry. India's wool textile production was based on only thirty mills in 1922; Japan's industry was deemed to be 'not good enough to compete with British woollens for

Figure 2 Exports of Wool Manufacturers, United Kingdom, 1900–1938

Source: Mitchell and Deane, Table 8, p. 396.

which Japan is Great Britain's best market' given the difficulties that industry was experiencing in blending and mixing wool fibres.[9]

There is one crucial respect in which the performance of the woollen industry differs markedly from that of cotton: output levels in the major branches of the woollen industry displayed a much greater resilience to demand shocks than was the case in the cotton industry (Table 1). Although both industries faced major declines in their export markets, the impact of the decline was less severe in the woollen than in the cotton industry. Unlike the cotton industry, the domestic market was to become important as a sales outlet for the woollen industry. Why was this?

One possibility was that the two industries had very different industrial structures. Such a view, which is well established in the business

Table 1 Percentage Decline in Production of Cotton and Wool, 1912–1938

Cotton Manufactures	*Cotton Yarn*	*Woollen Tissues*	*Woollen Yarn*
–53	–41	–8.7	–6

Source: The data for cotton have been estimated from B. R. Mitchell and Phyllis Deane, *Abstract of British Historical Statistics*. The data for wool apply to the period 1912 to 1935 and have been estimated using Board of Trade, *Wool*, p. 5.

history literature, contends that one of the key features determining industrial success during the twentieth century, was the ability to effect 'the three-pronged investment in production, distribution, and management, essential to exploit economies of scale and scope.'[10] For Chandler, as with Lazonick,[11] a symbiotic relationship exists between the strategies that firms are able to pursue and their internal structure.

However, even the most cursory of examinations of the two industries during the inter-war years is sufficient to discount structural factors as an explanation for differential performance. Both industries possessed remarkably similar structures, with high degrees of geographical and product specialisation, together with a preponderance of small firms in each stage of production.

The geographical specialisation which existed in the cotton industry is well documented. This division, by which spinning was largely concentrated in the south and west, and weaving largely concentrated in the north and east of Lancashire, was reinforced by product specialisation. In spinning, for example, high-count yarn production was concentrated on Bolton, Leigh, and Manchester. Coarse and medium count production was concentrated on Oldham and Rochdale. In weaving, the towns of Colne and Nelson specialised in the production of fine coloured goods; Burnley was engaged mainly on medium grey cloths for export to the East, and Blackburn and Darwen concentrated on fine grey cloths for the Indian market.[12] This pattern of geographic and product specialisation, which existed in Lancashire's cotton industry, was mirrored in the Yorkshire woollen industry. Halifax and Keighley specialised in the production of a variety of worsted yarns and dress goods, Dewsbury and Batley were the main centres of the heavy woollen district making a variety of goods ranging from low woollens to good quality men's wear as well as rugs and blankets, whilst Leeds had both worsted and woollen activities ranging from fine cloth to plain woollen goods. Huddersfield produced fine woollen cloths as well as high quality worsteds for men's wear.[13]

Both industries were also remarkably similar in terms of industrial concentration. In 1930 over 60 per cent of returns in cotton to the Census were made by firms which employed less than 200 workers. These firms accounted for nearly a quarter of all those employed and of net output in cotton spinning.[14] Large firms, i.e. those employing over 1,000, by contrast accounted for less than one per cent of the total returns, 14 per cent of net output and 10.6 per cent of employment. Small scale undertakings were prevalent in nearly all branches, with the large majority being privately owned and conducted businesses. In the early 1920s, 56.4 per cent of the 1,384 companies in wool textiles were private firms and, of those, 78.6 per cent employed less than 100 people.[15] This was to remain the dominant structure throughout the inter-war years.[16] By 1935, two-thirds of all workers were employed in the 1,435 factories that employed less than 500 workers.[17]

It is apparent from the above that both industries contained highly specialised, but fragmented structures. Firms in both industries were also highly competitive, ruinously so in the cotton industry. Crucially, however, there was a major difference in the way in which this competition manifested itself. Whereas cotton is characterised as having an ethos of 'traditional individualism' which had 'dissipated the dwindling resources of the industry in bitter internecine warfare between sections and in cut-throat competition between firms',[18] the woollen industry chose to concentrate its efforts on market segmentation, where competitive energies were directed to building up demand in market niches. In addition, cotton textiles tried to evolve collusive strategies which entailed centralised decisions and bargaining. Collusion took two forms: price and labour rationing. For collusion to operate entailed collective centralised decision making and the constant threat for firms to break away. Wool, by contrast, placed much less emphasis upon collusive practices, especially from the mid-1920s, and this provided greater opportunities for decision making to be devolved to individual firms (see Sections IV and V below for how and why this occurred).

Structural factors do not appear to have been key determinants of industrial performance. Conduct variables may explain the very different performances of the two industries. We argue that there were three major areas in which the conduct of firms in the woollen industry differed from those in cotton. These were marketing policies, the absence of speculative reflotations during the 1919–1921 boom, and a distinct pattern of labour organisation. Taken together, these three aspects of conduct separated the woollen industry from the cotton industry and ensured that it was the former and not the latter which was able to weather the storm of the inter-war years.

III.

Trade theories help to place the inter-war cotton and woollen industries in a long-run global context. In these terms, the ideas inherent in the product cycle theory of trade are particularly useful. This theory postulates a dynamic evolution of comparative advantage, with the source of exports shifting through the life cycle of the product. Early on in the cycle, the innovating country (in this case the UK's cotton and woollen industries), accounts for an important, if not dominant, share of world exports of the good but is then displaced by other developed countries, which in turn are ultimately displaced as production processes become disseminated to less developed countries. Capital and labour costs play a crucial role. Because capital is more mobile than labour, the price of capital across countries will diverge less than the price of labour. Countries having lower labour costs will thus be able to undercut the innovating country. This is especially the case, as in textiles, where labour costs are a substantial part of total production costs.

Two implications follow from this. First, if the textile industries in the innovating country are to survive on *any* scale, then they need to concentrate on high-quality, high-income markets where price (and therefore labour costs) are of secondary importance. In order for such a strategy to succeed, effort has to be directed to the output of high value-added products for niche markets. But this is not sufficient in itself. Since technology is quickly disseminated throughout advanced industrial economies, it follows that such economies will also have access to the same technology. If the innovating country is to succeed by exporting to these countries, it must also try to contain its labour costs. From this perspective, control of labour costs is no longer a substitute for product innovation but a necessary corollary if the innovating country is to penetrate high-income markets.

Wool textiles pursued a policy of pursuing high-quality niche market specialisation aimed at developed markets. As world demand shifted in the more highly developed countries from lower grade goods to those of a higher class, wool adapted its production strategy. Exports of low grade goods declined, to be replaced by those of finer grade goods.[19] Overseas, many old markets were retained and new ones developed, largely as a result of market niche specialisation in finer goods in the more highly developed countries.[20] The standard practice in the inter-war years was for firms in the industry to build up a reputation for quality in their own special lines in both home and export markets.[21] Product ranges were extended and new styles introduced.[22] As such, although exports to China and Japan fell, those to the developed economies of Europe, South Africa and the USA held up well. By contrast, the cotton industry was unable to make up for the loss of its principal, Indian, market and singularly failed to adopt wool's product niche specialisation and developed markets strategy.

The woollen textile industry, however, did not depend on overseas markets alone for its relative prosperity. Had wool relied entirely or even mainly on export demand, the industry would have faced ruin.

Even with the product niche strategy, survival could not be guaranteed via export demand. Specialisation into developed export markets cushioned the industry against the kind of collapse experienced by cotton textiles, but it was not sufficient to sustain the industry. Survival depended to a large extent on the industry's strategy of developing the home market.

Prior to 1914, clothes retailing for men was dominated by two sectors, bespoke and ready to wear. The former involved a number of visits by the customer to the tailor for a series of fittings to ensure the made-to-measure garment had an accurate fitting. Naturally, such clothes were very expensive. The ready-to-wear article, as its name implies, involved 'off-the-peg' clothes. Such items may not fit as well as the made-to-measure article, but they are much cheaper. Before 1914, there had been a small move toward wholesale bespoke tailoring initiated by Hepworths and another Leeds based clothier, William Blackburn.[23] The defining characteristic of the wholesale bespoke trade was that it produced ready-to-wear clothes which, with a few minor alterations at the factory premises, could be made to have the appearance of made to measure. However, the marketing problem confronting the wholesale bespoke trade was more complex: the wholesale bespoke trade had to be able to compete on quality with the bespoke trade and, simultaneously, compete on price with the ready-to-wear trade.[24]

The end of the First World War, and the demobilisation of over two million soldiers, offered the prospect for the rapid expansion of wholesale bespoke tailoring by the multiple clothing retailers. Burtons, together with Hepworths were to be the key players in this trend. Aggressive marketing policies and powerful advertising campaigns generated a growing demand for wholesale bespoke clothes.[25] This demand was channelled, via their own factories, to the woollen and worsted industry in Yorkshire. These retailers were acutely aware of the potential offered by the domestic market, and it was this awareness, supported by Chandlerian investments in production and marketing, which explain why, despite a serious fall in exports, output in the woollen industry held up much better than in cotton. Indeed, by 1937, the home market absorbed nearly 70 per cent of tissue output.[26]

The sales policies of these retailers were to be central to the cultivation of the domestic market. The contribution of the major clothing retailers to the fortunes of the woollen industry cannot be under-estimated. By the 1940s, major clothing manufacturers consumed between 53 per cent and 77 per cent of all cloth deliveries intended for clothing in the domestic market. The higher figure quoted here estimates consumption as a percentage of total-utility deliveries;

the lower figure estimates consumption as a percentage of the total of utility and non-utility deliveries.[27] Expressed as a percentage of the industry's total output, deliveries of cloth to the major clothing manufacturers is no less impressive: cloth consumed by these manufacturers accounted for between 22 per cent and 35 per cent of the industry's *total* output in the 1930s.[28] In a very real sense, the activities of these retailers were pivotal to the fortunes of the woollen industry during the inter-war years. The time and effort expended by the wool textile industry in 'modern' marketing methods underpinned the successful development of the domestic market: a strategy which cotton seemed unable and unwilling to adopt.

Indeed, as Broadberry and Marrison have recently claimed, a principal explanation for the failure of cotton firms to invest in mass-distribution technques related directly to the availability of market information and other services provided by Manchester and Liverpool merchants and brokers who dominated the industry.[29] This affected the transaction costs associated with internalising the function. Wool also had its merchants and brokers. It also had to consider the costs of internalising the function within the individual firm. But wool manufacturers and merchants appeared better able to communicate and keen to exploit the domestic and export markets afforded by the product niche specialisation strategy.

IV.

One of the defining characteristics of many of the UK's staple industries during the inter-war years was the persistence of substantial excess capacity.[30] The standard interpretation of this phenomenon is that in response to an export boom in the years immediately preceding the First World War, the staple industries increased their capacity. However, during the inter-war years, as a result of a series of exogenous demand shocks, exports were at a much lower level than they were pre-1914, and the UK's staple industries had a glut of capacity.

This interpretation fits the experiences of the cotton. In response to an intermittent export boom between 1900–1913, when exports increased by over 40 per cent, capacity in the cotton spinning and weaving industries was increased by approximately 40 and 21 per cent, respectively.[31] During the inter-war years, according to contemporary estimates, as a result of the collapse of exports, the industry was saddled with excess capacity.[32]

The interpretation does not apply very well to the woollen industry. Total exports of all wool manufactures (excluding blankets and carpets) increased by just 10 per cent 1900–1913, with gains in exports in one sector (woollen tissues) being largely offset by decline in others (worsted tissues).[33] Accordingly, this industry was not subject to the same hysterical bursts of capacity expansion which so characterised the cotton industry, and therefore it did not have to confront the issue of excess capacity on the same scale.

Exclusive focus upon exogenous demand shocks overlooks the possibility that the differential response of the two industries may have been adversely affected by endogenous shocks. Of particular interest in this context was the response of the two industries to the post-war boom. We argue below that the extent and nature of the re-capitalisation boom 1919–1921, in the cotton spinning industry, not only adversely affected its financial health but also severely limited the strategies it could adopt. By contrast, the woollen industry was largely immune from the re-capitalisation boom and this fact alone automatically gave the industry the opportunity to adopt a much wider range of competitive strategies.

Increasingly, in the economics literature, there has been a growing awareness of the problems facing firms whose investments have a large element of sunk costs.[34] The presence of these costs affects both the investment and exit decision of firms. For example, when deciding whether or not to invest, firms have to be reasonably certain that they are going to be able to recoup their expenditures. In an economic environment which is very uncertain, it may be more sensible for firms to delay investment expenditures which, once undertaken, cannot be undone easily. Conversely, when investment expenditures have been undertaken and the economic environment *ex post* turns out to be less favourable than anticipated, the battle for financial survival becomes all the more acute. On the one hand, firms cannot simply exit the industry (and thereby incur losses on their existing investment expenditures) while, on the other hand, the strategies they adopt must necessarily be subsumed to recouping these expenditures.

Such insights suggest that badly timed investment expenditures and/or too much expenditure can generate hysteresis in an industry. It follows that industries which suffer from hysteresis are at a comparative disadvantage compared with industries that do not. In this respect, the difference in competitive strategies between the cotton and woollen industries during the inter-war years was most marked.

In the pre-1914 period, high levels of profit in the cotton industry had been a signal to expand capacity. During the 1919–1921 boom, however, the response of cotton firms was to refloat themselves: owners of spinning firms issued new shares in their company and these were bought by speculators at a high price in the expectation of forming a new company with a capitalisation based on the exceptional profits that were being made and which they thought were likely to continue.[35] Between August 1919 and April 1920, the *average* price paid per 1,000 spindles increased from £1,400 to £4,160.[36] A total of 217 companies in the spinning industry, and 110 firms in the weaving industry were involved in this boom. Between them, these firms accounted for 46 and 14 per cent, respectively, of their industry's capacity.[37]

The method used to finance the reflotation compounded the problems. Shareholders were called upon to provide only 55 per cent of the finance, the remainder being raised by loans, bank overdrafts and debentures. This latter observation is especially pertinent because this finance bears fixed interest which has to be paid irrespective of whether profits are being made. Effectively, the means used to finance the reflotation augmented the fixed costs of the industry.

The woollen industry was not immune from the post-war reflotation boom. Like the cotton industry, it was recognised that exceptional profits were made in the immediate post-war years. Investigations into the woollen industry were made compulsory under the Profiteering Acts, in 1920 and 1921. These investigations revealed the following trends. In the wool top and yarn making industry, the average profit per pound (weight) was fifteen times the pre-war figure.[38] This corresponded to an increase in net profits as a percentage of total capital employed from 15.7 per cent in 1912 to 59.44 per cent in 1919.[39] It was reported that one firm in 1919 had made a profit of 88.8 per cent of capital employed, and this was after deduction of Excess Profits Duty. In the worsted yarn industry, profits per pound (weight) increased from 1d to 3d (during the control period) to between 8.5d and 34.5d per pound after control.[40] In the tweed cloth industry, it was reported that net profit on sales had increased from an average of 10.1 per cent during the pre-war years to 19.7 per cent in 1919.[41]

The scale on which this boom occurred, however, was much smaller than in the cotton industry. The primary reason for this was the preponderance of private firms. In 1926, 56 per cent of firms in the woollen industry were private firms.[42] This figure should be regarded as a considerable under-estimate given the number of companies which did not issue shares. According to the Committee on Industry and Trade, many of the 603 firms described as limited liability companies were, in fact, private companies.[43] Moreover, according to evidence given before the Court of Enquiry (1925), there were only fifteen publicly quoted companies in existence and it is not clear that all of these were reflotations (Table 2).[44]

Table 2 Recapitalisations in the Wool Industry

Company	*Registered*	*Paid up Capital*	*Recapitalisations*
A & S Henry & Co. Ltd.	3.12.1889	1,700,000	April 1920: 640,000 at £1.5 per share
Colbeck Bros. Ltd.	22.11.1889	125,000	None
Crowe & Co. Ltd.	3.1.1900	100,000	May 1919: 75,000 at £1
Woolcombers Ltd.	12.12.1904	300,000	Several rights issues : 1918
Willey & Pearson	9.5.1895	60,000	None
Heckmondwike Manufacturing Co. Ltd.	10.1.1900	81,210	None
Lister & Co.	20.2.1889	1,425,000	None
M. Oldroyd & Sons Ltd.	10.5.1920	200,000	None
Geo. H. Hirst & Co. Ltd.	1.3.1920	160,000	None
Huddersfield Fine Worsteds Ltd.	28.10.1920	321,433	None
Illingworth Morris & Co. Ltd.	18.2.1920	46,216	September 1923
Francis Wiley & Co. Ltd.	9.10.1919	188,056	None
Patons and Baldwins	16.4.1920	1,599,291	None
Salts (Saltaire) Ltd.	12.6.1923	1,000,000	None
Smith, Bulmer & Co. Ltd.	9.5.1923	1,121,344	None

Source: Bradford Archive Office Transcript of Court of Investigation into the Wool Textile Industry, Vol. 2, 3D86: 9/2/5, Tuesday 22 September 1925.

A crucial difference between the two industries was that of debt incurred as a result of their reflotation strategies. The cotton industry as a whole saddled itself with large amounts of fixed interest bearing debt as a result of its reflotation strategies. There was some reflotation in wool, but on nothing like the same scale as that in cotton. The industries entered the beginning of the inter-war years with markedly different debt structures. This was to have important repercussions for subsequent strategy.

The difference between cotton and wool lay not in re-equipment policy but in debt. There was some contraction in the wool industry (between 1918 and 1938 there was a contraction in the woollen industry from 6,459,000 to 5,493,000 spinning spindles and from 115,000 to 78,000 power looms),[45] but this was far less than that in cotton, given the absence of rationalisation in the former industry. Rationalisation was negated by a policy in wool which stressed market niches and product differentation. Nor did wool engage in heavy investment in new machinery: a quarter of worsted spindles were installed before 1900 and many of the looms in use in the inter-war years were over fifty years old. There was no real incentive to re-equip as most of the machinery was extremely durable and could produce with comparative efficiency for over fifty years.[46] Some wool carding machines had been in existence for over eighty years.[47] The implications are illustrated by the relative performance of wool and cotton textiles in terms of capacity. Between 1900 and 1913, capacity in the spinning and weaving sections of the cotton industry increased by almost 40 per cent and 21 per cent, respectively.[48] In the woollen industry a very different rate of capacity expansion was evident. Between 1904 and 1918, spinning and weaving capacity increased by just 14 and 26 per cent, respectively.[49]

The combination of a limited contraction and the lack of any incentive to re-equip meant there was no major investment programme in wool. The difference lay in relative debt rather than investment and the implications of the former for the subsequent ability of the industries to weather the depressed conditions of the inter-war years. Because the scale and nature of the reflotation boom (and hence debt) was larger in the cotton industry it followed that the associated uncertainty and financial pressures were greater than in the woollen industry. The consequence of this was that all firms in the cotton industry had to consider themselves financially vulnerable and potentially marginal.[50] This, in turn, generated defensive pressures to pursue collective decision making, especially on the key issues of industry output (regulated by collective short-time working) and industry price (regulated by industry-wide price associations). By contrast, the woollen industry did not experience these pressures to the same extent or severity. This, in turn, allowed much greater scope for firms to pursue their own individual strategies, unconstrained by the need to observe any collective policy.

V.

In the previous section we argued that higher levels of financial fragility increased uncertainty in the cotton industry compared with the woollen industry. The consequence of this was that there was a more pressing need for the cotton industry to effect collective, industry-wide agreements, on prices and output. There was, in addition, a third variable, labour costs, whose management was also affected by the differing need to pursue collective agreements in the two industries. Whereas the centralisation and collectivisation of wage setting dogged the attempts of cotton textiles to control wage costs, wool was able to pursue individualistic labour rationing and wage control at the firm level which, in turn, reflected the decentralisation of the wage setting.

At the beginning of the inter-war period, both the cotton and woollen textile industries operated on a centralised, collective wage bargaining basis. To a large extent, this collectivisation was both inevitable and necessary during the war years when there was a need to avoid industrial unrest. Indeed, in the woollen industry, this collectivisation was enshrined under the auspices of a Joint Industrial Council which received widespread support from both employers and workers alike.[51] However, it was in the inter-war period itself, especially after the ending of the post-war boom in 1921, that the two industries diverged markedly in their pursuit of collective wage bargaining.

In the cotton spinning industry widespread financial fragility threatened the very survival of the industry: there was a pervasive fear that 'weak selling' would ruin all firms, both the technically strong (but financially weak) and the technically weak (and financially weak). Since profits are the difference between selling price and costs of production (and since labour costs were a large part of total production costs), it followed that collective action was necessary not only on prices, but also on wages. Control of wages in the industry was to be effected by organised, industry-wide, short-time working.[52]

Organised short-time working in the cotton spinning industry, however, at best yielded only marginal benefits and, at worst, exacerbated the problems of price competitiveness in the industry. One problem was that there was always an incentive for the most marginal firms to break away from the agreed amount of short-time working and supply more orders by themselves, at the expense of their counterparts. A further problem was that short-time working, by increasing the amount of capacity under-utilisation, worked to increase unit costs of production which exacerbated the industry's general price competitiveness. This latter issue was especially damaging for firms which had recently re-equipped and whose price competitiveness depended on operating capacity to the maximum possible extent. In effect, the viability of the minority (the most modern firms) was being sacrificed to protect the majority (the financially weak). Not surprisingly, as conditions deteriorated in this industry, less emphasis was placed on controlling operating costs through organised short-time working, and more emphasis was placed on controlling the final selling price.[53]

In a similar vein, efforts to achieve consensus and industry-wide agreements in the weaving industry undermined, and then nullified, the efforts of firms trying to become more competitive by increasing loom allocations (the More Looms Experiment, hereafter, MLS).[54] Like the cotton spinning industry, the weaving industry suffered from unviable costs of production. In an attempt to improve competitiveness, some firms were willing to adopt the MLS. But this threatened to undermine the competitiveness of firms which, for a variety of reasons (such as type of cloth produced) were unable to adopt the system. In order to pacify these latter firms, and in order to try and prevent the industry being plunged into chaos, the industry's leaders sought to improve the competitiveness of these firms by lowering the wage rates they had to pay their workers. However, the almost ludicrous outcome, which was enshrined by 1935, was that costs of MLS increased and the costs of non-MLS were reduced. In the weaving industry, the desire to preserve consensus and solidarity had the effect of undermining any scheme to improve price competitiveness.[55]

For the cotton spinning and weaving industries, therefore, emphasis upon collectivisation had the effect of generating paralysis … The need to preserve consensus nullified the efforts of individual firms which sought to improve their competitiveness. Moreover, collective strategies of cost containment through organised short-time working had a limited effect. Cost containment via the wage rate was far more successful in wool than in cotton (Figure 3), Unit labour costs did fall in cotton textiles, but they were somewhat erratic The contrast provided by the wool industry could not be more marked or instructive.

We have already indicated that collective action was widely supported in the woollen industry during the First World War. This made

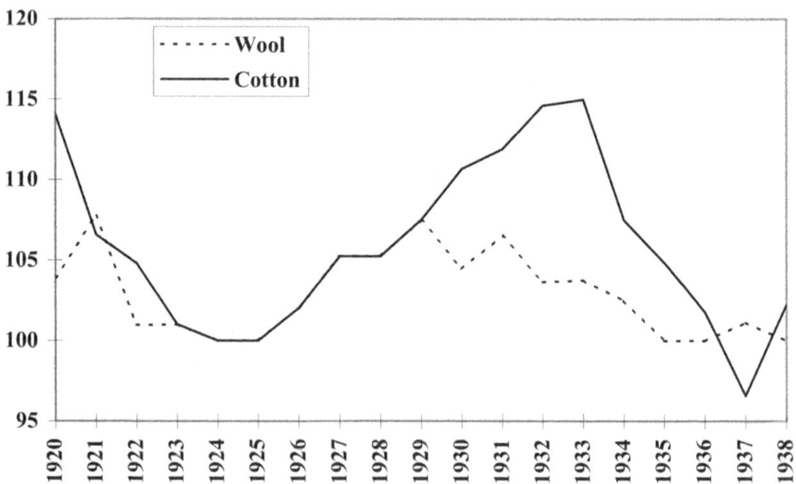

Figure 3 Index of Real Weekly Wage Rates in the Inter-War Textile Industries

Source: Estimated from Mitchell and Deane.

sense when all firms confronted similar problems. However, when the trading environment confronting each section of the industry become more varied following the ending of the post-war boom in 1921, much less effort was devoted to trying to maintain industry-wide solidarity in the industry.[56] The immediate benefit of this was that firms did not have to subsume their individual competitive strategies to issues such as prices, output and wage rates, which were of industry-wide concern.

It is true that industry-wide consensus did exist among employers in all sections of the woollen industry in the early 1920s, especially on the issue of wage cuts. For example, in the couple of years preceding the 1925 Court of Inquiry into the woollen industry, there had been growing dissatisfaction among employers generally about the level of wages which had been granted during propitious wartime conditions[57] but which, in the depressed conditions of the early 1920s, came to look increasingly anomalous.

However, it is also well documented that an industry as complex as the woollen and worsted industries can have very disparate economic fortunes at each point in time and through time. And indeed, where production processes where vertically specialised it is easy to imagine that gains in one section of the trade were at the expense of those further down the chain. Moreover, fundamental differences between the woollen and worsted sections of the industry were important to the way in which employers in each section viewed their commercial interests. Compared with worsted manufacturers, both woollen and worsted spinners had a much greater range of potential buyers, many of which were not necessarily vertically related. For example, at each stage of worsted yarn production the product was marketable so that the market for the intermediate products did not necessarily lie in the subsequent stage of domestic manufacture. However, manufacturers of worsted cloths were almost entirely dependent on domestically produced yarns and, as export markets collapsed, they became increasingly dependent on the fortunes of the domestic market.[58]

Signs of this disunity had been apparent in the period preceding the 1925 Court of Inquiry. For example, Bradford manufacturers had wanted to begin negotiations at 20 per cent and were adamant that their trade would not bear anything less than 10 per cent.[59] Spinning federations, however, who were enjoying, and would *continue* to enjoy relatively more buoyant export markets, were reluctant to support a wage reduction if this involved enforcing a lockout.[60] However, a general (but fragile) consensus was achieved because of the recognition of the consequences which would follow if both sides of the employers decided 'to go it alone'.[61]

From the late 1920s, however, the consensus which existed between the employers began to break down. The breakdown in the (fragile) consensus which existed during the early 1920s came about as more fundamental differences in the economic fortunes confronting each individual sector and region came to the forefront. Of particular importance in this respect, was the growing divergence between the interests of spinners and manufacturers. As trade deteriorated throughout the 1920s, fragility increased. The main fault line was between spinners and manufacturers. Spinners, especially woollen spinners, tended to do much better in export markets than manufacturers.[62]

For manufacturers, however, the export situation was disastrous. Although their saviour was in the domestic market as wholesale bespoke retailing accelerated, it was not the case that the domestic market could save all sections of the manufacturing industry. Generally speaking, it was the fine worsted centres – especially Huddersfield – which stood to do very well out of the domestic market. Massive changes in fashion, in favour of lighter more sophisticated cloths for blazers, suits, and sports jackets, favoured Huddersfield and Leeds clothes producers. By contrast, other woollen and worsted centres, especially Bradford, Halifax and Keighley, produced a much wider range of materials, were less able to benefit from the fashion changes in the domestic market, and were generally the most vociferous in their demand for wage reductions.

Clearly, given the widespread differences in trading conditions facing each sector of the woollen industry, there was much less incentive to pursue collective action on wages. In the woollen industry, unlike the cotton industry, there was much greater recognition of the different economic conditions facing each sector and much greater acceptance that collective action on wages could never generate satisfactory outcomes. This being the case, each section of the industry and individual firms in each section, had much greater scope for pursuing their own strategies which were tailored to their own specific circumstances.

The outcome in terms of control of labour costs was much more successful than in either section of the cotton industry. Except for 1937 and a brief period in 1921, weekly wage rates in woollen textiles were far lower than those in cotton textiles (Figure 3). Unit labour costs undoubtedly fell in both industries as wage rates were driven down, but wool appears to have been able to achieve unit costs far lower than those of the cotton industry. By 1935, our estimates indicate unit labour costs of £0.96 in cotton textiles, but £0.02 in wool.[63] Productivity, moreover, in the woollen textile industry surpassed that of cotton by the mid-1930s (Table 3).

Table 3 The Performance of the Woollen and Cotton Textile Industries, 1935

	Gross Output £000s	*Net Output per Person Employed £*	*Number of Establishments*
Cotton spinning & doubling	74,475	111.00	820
Cotton weaving	60,301	122.00	884
Woollens	33,144	173.37	596
Worsted woollens	64,444	172.67	617

Source: Census of Production, 1951, Summary Tables, Part I, Table 1, p. 16

VI.

This paper has sought to explain the different performance of the cotton and woollen industries. We recognise that a part, but only a small part, of the difference in performance between the two industries can be explained by the different impact of exogenous shocks. There should be no doubt that cotton manufactures and cotton spinners confronted much bigger declines in their export markets than their counterparts in the woollen industry.

Exogenous shocks only form part of the story. The woollen industry was relatively successful because in three key aspects of conduct, its behaviour differed from that of cotton. The woollen industry adopted a much more aggressive sales policy, both in export markets and in the domestic market. Niche marketing in foreign markets, and sales promotion and multiple retailing in the domestic market was one way in which the policy of wool differed from that of cotton. The second aspect of behaviour was the absence of speculative reflotations which served to minimise financial fragility and uncertainty in the industry. From this and finally, the industry, unlike cotton, had no incentive to pursue collective centralised bargaining. That, in turn, allowed firm level wage setting and labour rationing which allowed the industry to contain its variable costs.

Two key conclusions emerge from this paper. The first is that too much emphasis can be given to exogenous shocks as determinants of relative industrial performance. Endogenous shocks, such as debilitating over-capitalisation and speculative reflotation can have just as profound adverse effects. Indeed, to the extent that such shocks can generate hysteresis effects, their consequences may last much longer than short, but violent, changes in export markets. The second conclusion is that it need not automatically follow that because an industry has suffered a major exogenous shock it is necessarily doomed. The inter-war performance of the woollen industry provides ample testimony to this.

Glossary of technical terms

Carding: The object of the carding process is to open up the raw wool and make the fibres parallel to some extent.

Tops: Once the wool has been carded it is sent for combing which further assists in the parallelisation of fibre. The continuous progression of the wool through combing results in a straightening of the longer fibres which are drawn off as a continuous sliver known as the 'top'.

Noils: These are the shorter wool fibres which result from combing.

Woollen and Worsted yarns: The difference between these two, lies primarily in the manufacturing processes employed. In the worsted section of the industry, wool, together with other fibres such as mohair and alpaca, go through a series of processes (including combing), of which the main intermediate processes are tops and yarns. In the woollen section, a wider range of materials, including not only raw wool but also fibres recovered from rags, is spun into yarn without the production of any intermediate products. As a general rule, there is much more consistency in the length of fibre employed in the worsted section than in the woollen section.

Source: Board of Trade, *Wool*, p. 7, and Appendix VIII (p. 221).

Notes

* We are grateful to Chris Wrigley for first imparting his infectious enthusiasm for research on wool textiles, to John Wilson for sterling editorial encouragement and advice, to Quentin Outram for perceptive comments on short-time working in the inter-war 'staple' industries, to Andy Marrison and Tim Leunig for their awkward questions on cotton textiles and to the archivists at the Bradford Archive Office for their patience and help in our fieldwork. This research was supported by a Hallsworth Fellowship (Sue Bowden) and a Nuffield grant (Dave Higgins).

1. Wool textiles recorded a drop in employment from 1912 to 1937 of 30,000 (or 11 per cent), whereas cotton textiles recorded a fall of 260,000 (42 per cent). Production of tops remained stable throughout the inter-war years, yarn output actually increased and tissues, after experiencing decline in the early post-war years and again in 1930–1 recovered thereafter. By 1937, the output in terms of weight or area was very close to that of 1912. Board of Trade, *Wool* (London, 1947), pp. 338.042, pp. 4–5.
2. By far the best and the only economic survey of the industry which surveys the many aspects of its long history is George Rannie (ed.), *The Woollen and Worsted Industry: An Economic Analysis* (Oxford: Clarendon, 1965). Another good overview is provided by A. Brearley, *The Woollen Industry* (1965). Allen surveys the industry in G. C. Allen, *British Industries and Their Organisation* (London: Longman, 5th ed., 1970), whilst Lucas

examines collusive tendencies in Arthur Fletcher Lucas, *Industrial Reconstruction and the Control of Competition: The British Experiment* (London: Longman, 1937). The most recent work on the industry in the nineteenth and twentieth century which looks at industrial relations, rather than the economics of employment strategies in the inter-war years, is contained in three chapters of J. A. Jowett and A. J. McIvor (eds), *Employers and Labour in the English Textile Industries, 1859–1939* (London, 1988).

3. A. R. Burnett-Hurst, 'Lancashire and the Indian market', *Journal of the Royal Statistical Society*, Vol. 95 (1932), p. 398.
4. Burnett-Hurst, 'Lancashire', p. 410.
5. B. Ellinger and H. Ellinger, 'Japanese competition in the cotton trade', *Journal of the Royal Statistical Society*, Vol. 93 (1930), pp. 185–218.
6. For example, between late 1923 and early 1925, there was an exceptional increase in British exports of all classes of woollen tissues to the Far East. The cause of this boom was over-buying by Japanese merchants with the intent of re-exporting to China. G. H. Wood, 'Essay on changes in the distribution of British overseas trade in wool textiles during the past ten years', *Weltwirtschaftliches Archiv.*, Vol. 33 (1931), pp. 503–29.
7. Committee on Industry and Trade, *Survey of the Textile Industries* (1928), p. 174.
8. Board of Trade, *Wool*, pp. 5–6.
9. Bradford Archive Office (hereinafter BAO), Transcript of Court of Investigation into the Wool Textile Industry, Vol. 1, 3D86/9/2/5, Monday 21 September 1925, p. 37–38.
10. Alfred D. Chandler, Jr., *Scale and Scope: The Dynamics of Industrial Capitalism* (Cambridge, Mass.: Belknap Press, 1990), p. 286.
11. For example, W. A. Lazonick, 'The cotton industry' in B. Elbaum and W. A. Lazonick (eds), *The Decline of the British Economy* (Oxford: Oxford University Press, 1987), pp. 39–45. As far as the cotton industry is concerned, recent work has questioned the financial justification for greater vertical integration. See, for example, D. M. Higgins and S. Toms, 'Firm structure and financial performance: the Lancashire textile industry, c. 1884-c. 1960', *Accounting, Business and Financial History*, Vol. 7 (1997), pp. 195–232.
12. For a discussion of this geographical specialisation see, for example, S. Kenny, 'Sub-regional specialisation in the Lancashire cotton industry, 1884–1914: a study in organisational and locational change', *Journal of Historical Geography*, Vol. 8 (1982), pp. 41–63.
13. Board of Trade, *Wool*, pp. 2–3; BAO, Arnold Frobisher, *Report on Wages in the Woollen and Worsted Industries, 1880–1920*, 20D81: 78, pp. 17, 18, 22.
14. Board of Trade, Census of Production, *Final Report on the Fourth Census of Production, Part I: The Textile Trades* (1933), p. 32.
15. Committee on Industry and Trade, *Survey*, pp. 175–6.
16. Board of Trade, *Wool*, p. 15.
17. Board of Trade, Census of Production (London, 1935).
18. Lucas, *Industrial Reconstruction*, pp. 146 and 150.
19. BAO, Minutes of a Court of Inquiry into the matters in dispute between the parties to the Northern Counties District Wool (and Allied) Textile Industrial Council, Vol. 1, 3D86/9/3/1, 27 January 1930, p. 88.

20. BAO, Minutes of a Court of Inquiry into the matters in dispute between the parties to the Northern Counties District Wool (and Allied) Textile Industrial Council, Vol. 1, 3D86/9/3/1, 27 January 1930, pp. 87–8.
21. Committee on Industry and Trade, *Survey*, p. 184.
22. Board of Trade, *Wool*, p. 15.
23. These firms began as clothiers and integrated forward to own their own retailing premises. By such means they were able to supply their products directly to the public rather than through a middleman. Many other Leeds clothiers, for example, John Barran & Son, and Messrs Buckley & Son, remained wholesale clothiers, supplying their goods to the public via merchants. J. Thomas, 'A history of the Leeds clothing industry', *Yorkshire Bulletin of Economic and Social Research*, Occasional Paper No. 1 (1955), p. 48.
24. Thomas, 'history of Leeds clothing', p. 51.
25. Between 1921 and 1938, the number of people employed in the Leeds tailoring industry increased from 24,979, to 51,025. Thomas, 'History of Leeds clothing', p. 54. The marketing strategy of Burtons during this period is discussed in K. Honeyman, 'Montague Burton Ltd: The creators of well dressed men', in J. Chartres and K. Honeyman (eds), *Leeds City Business* (Leeds, 1993) pp. 186–216, and in E. M. Sigsworth, *Montague Burton: the Tailor of Taste* (Manchester: Manchester University Press, 1990), pp. 30–56.
26. Board of Trade, *Wool*, Table 15, p. 23.
27. Calculated from Board of Trade, *Wool*, Table 59, p. 213. The higher figure is obtained by expressing consumption as a percentage of total-utility deliveries. The lower figure is obtained by expressing consumption as a percentage of the total of utility and non-utility deliveries.
28. The only date for which we can get information on the delivery of cloth to the major retailers is 1944. The data show that in this year cloth retailers took deliveries of approximately 58.1 million *linear* yards (Board of Trade, *Wool*, p. 213). Average production per year in the 1930s was approximately 417 million *square* yards. In order to calculate deliveries as a percentage of production, we need to know the width of cloth produced. The maximum width of a standard loom in this period was ninety inches (exactly 2.5 yards). This implies that clothing retailers took 35 per cent of production. It has been stated that the average width of cloth actually produced during this period would have been around 56 inches, or 1.5 yards (this is very similar to estimates given in Balfour, p. 195). This implies that the clothing retailers took 22 per cent of production. We are grateful to Douglas Bland, Department of Textiles, Huddersfield University, for providing information which enabled us to do these calculations.
29. S. N. Broadberry and A. Marrison, 'External economies of scale in the Lancashire cotton industry, 1900–1939, Paper presented at the Northern Economic History Conference, 10 November 1998.
30. See, for example, S. Bowden and D. M. Higgins, 'Short-time working and price maintenance: collusive tendencies in the cotton spinning industry, 1919–1939', *Economic History Review* (1998), pp. 319–43; F. Geary, 'The emergence of mass unemployment: wages and employment in shipbuilding between the wars', *Cambridge Journal of Economics* Vol. 21 (1997), pp. 303–21.

31. Calculated from R. Robson, *The Cotton Industry in Britain* (London: Macmillan, 1957), Table 5, p. 340.
32. One estimate was that by 1935, there were 13.5 million surplus spindles in the industry. T. D. Barlow, 'Surplus capacity in the Lancashire cotton industry', *Manchester School*, Vol. 6 (1935), pp. 32–6.
33. Calculated from Mitchell and Deane, *Abstract*, p. 197.
34. See, especially, R. Pindyck and A. Dixit, *Investment under Uncertainty* (Princeton, Princeton University Press, 1993).
35. G. W. Daniels and J. Jewkes, 'The post-war depression in the Lancashire cotton industry', *Journal of the Royal Statistical Society* (1928), p. 170.
36. Daniels and Jewkes, 'Post-war depression', p. 172.
37. Daniels and Jewkes, 'Post-war depression', p. 174.
38. Labour Research Department, Material prepared for the National Association of Unions in the Textile Trades by the Labour Research Department in connection with the dispute in the Wool Textile Industry, 20 August 1925, Bradford Archive Office, File Ref 3D86: 9/2/1.
39. *Ibid.*
40. *Ibid.*
41. *Ibid.*
42. Committee on Industry and Trade, *Survey*, p. 176.
43. Committee on Industry and Trade, *Survey*, p. 176.
44. Labour Research Department, Material prepared for the National Association of Unions in the Textile Trades by the Labour Research Department in connection with the dispute in the Wool Textile Industry, 20 August 1925, Bradford Archive Office, File Ref 3D86: 9/2/1.3D86/9/2/1, Appendix One.
45. Mitchell and Deane, *Abstract*, p. 198.
46. Board of Trade, *Wool*, p. 76.
47. *Ibid.*
48. Calculated from Robson, *Cotton Industry*, Table 5, p. 340.
49. Calculated from Mitchell and Deane, *Abstract*, Table 17, p. 198.
50. Firms which had re-equipped had heavy fixed costs to bear. Firms which had refloated had incurred heavy fixed interest payments. Both these types of firms were vulnerable to 'weak selling' which threatened to set prices in the industry to ruinous levels. For a further discussion see Bowden and Higgins, 'Short-time working', pp. 326–32.
51. C. Wrigley, 'Cosy co-operation under strain: industrial relations in the Yorkshire woollen industry, 1919–39', *University of York, Borthwick Paper* (1987), No. 71.
52. Bowden and Higgins, 'Short-time working', pp. 326–38.
53. Bowden and Higgins, 'Short-time working', pp. 326–38.
54. The major works on this topic are: A. J. Bullen, The Cotton Spinners and Manufacturers Assoc. and the breakdown of the Collective Bargaining System 1928–35 (unpublished M.A. thesis, Warwick, 1980); A. and L. Fowler, *The History of the Nelson Weavers Association* (Lancashire, 1985); A. Fowler, 'Lancashire cotton trade unionism in the inter-war years', in Jowitt and McIvor, *Employers and Labour*; E. Hopwood, *The Lancashire Weavers Story* (1969); A. J. McIvor, 'Cotton employers' organisations and labour relations, 1890–1939', in Jowitt and McIvor, *Employers and Labour*; A. J. McIvor, *Organised Capital: Employers' associations and*

industrial relations in northern England, 1880–1939 (Cambridge, 1996); J. H. Riley, The More-Looms System and Industrial Relations in the Lancashire Cotton Manufacturing Industry, 1928–1935 (unpublished M.A. thesis, Manchester, 1981). For a recent reinterpretation see S. Bowden and D. M. Higgins, 'Productivity on the cheap? The 'More Looms' experiment and the Lancashire weaving industry, *Business History*. (July 1999).
55. Bowden and Higgins, 'Productivity on the cheap?'.
56. See Wrigley, 'Cosy co-operation'.
57. For example, in 1919, the employers had conceded a 10 per cent increase in wages and had agreed to a sliding system of wage increases based upon movements in the cost of living as published in the Ministry of Labour *Gazette*.
58. I. Magrath, 'Protecting the interests of the trade: wool, textile employers' organisations in the 1920s', in Jowitt and McIvor, *Employers and Labour*, p. 45–6.
59. Magrath, 'Protecting', pp. 52–3.
60. Indeed, before the 1925 Court of Inquiry, the spinners federations, were quite prepared to resign from the Employers Council rather than support the manufacturers.
61. Magrath, 'Protecting', p. 54.
62. Many foreign countries which concentrated on setting up their own worsted spinning plant preferred to import supplies of woollen yarn.
63. Value of gross output in 1935 taken from Board of Trade, Census of Production for 1951, Summary Tables, Part 1, Table 1, p. 16; data on total wages paid in both industries taken from Ministry of Labour, Ministry of Labour Gazette, monthly 1935. We are unable, given the absence of annual data on the value of production for the wool industry, to estimate annual series of unit labour costs.

Official Sources

Board of Trade, Census of Production (1935).

Board of Trade, Working Party Reports, *Wool* (1947), pp. 338.042.

Report of the Committee on Finance and Industry, July 1931, Cmd. 3987.

Final Report of the Committee on Industry and Trade, March 1929, Cmd. 3282.

Committee on Industry and Trade, Survey of Textile Industries, 1928. (no command number given).

Primary Sources

Bradford Chamber of Commerce, Journal 1919–1938, Bradford Archive Office, File Ref: 71D80:3.

Frobisher, Arnold, Report on Wages in the Woollen and Worsted Industries, 1880–1920, Bradford Archive Office, File Ref: 20D81:78

Huddersfield Woollen Manufactures and Spinners Association, Weavers Scale, 8 May 1883, Bradford Archive Office, Salts, *Correspondence*, File Ref: 48D87: 1/4/49.

Labour Research Department, Material prepared for the National Association of Unions in the Textile Trades by the Labour Research Department in connection with the dispute in the Wool Textile Industry, 20 August 1925, Bradford Archive Office, File Ref 3D86: 9/2/2.

Labour Research Department, Supplementary memorandum prepared by the Labour Research Department for the Woollen and Worsted Enquiry, 18 September 1925, Bradford Archive Office, File Ref 3D86: 9/2/3.

Minutes of a Court of Inquiry into the matters in dispute between the parties to the Northern Counties District Wool (and Allied) Textile Industrial Council, Volume 1, 27 January 1930, Bradford Archive Office, File Ref 3D86: 9/3/1.

Minutes of a Court of Inquiry into the matters in dispute between the parties to the Northern Counties District Wool (and Allied) Textile Industrial Council, Volume 2, 28 January 1930, Bradford Archive Office, File Ref 3D86: 9/3/2.

Minutes of a Court of Inquiry into the matters in dispute between the parties to the Northern Counties District Wool (and Allied) Textile Industrial Council, Volume 3, 29 January 1930, Bradford Archive Office, File Ref 3D86: 9/3/3.

National Association of Unions in the Textile Trade, Report of the Court of Investigation in the Wool Textile Industry, 1925, Bradford Archive Office, File Ref 3D86: 9/2/8.

Transcript of Court of Investigation into the Wool Textile Industry, Vol. 1, Monday 21 September 1925, Bradford Archive Office, File Ref 3D86: 9/2/4.

Transcript of Court of Investigation into the Wool Textile Industry, Vol. 2, Tuesday 22 September 1925, Bradford Archive Office, File Ref 3D86: 9/2/5.

Transcript of Court of Investigation into the Wool Textile Industry, Vol. 3, Wednesday 23 September 1925, Bradford Archive Office, File Ref 3D86: 9/2/6.

Transcript of Court of Investigation into the Wool Textile Industry, Vol. 4, Monday 19 October 1925, Bradford Archive Office, File Ref 3D86: 9/2/7.

Woollen and Worsted Trade Federation, Annual Reports of the General Council, 19222–1938, Bradford Archive Office, File Ref 20D81/4.

Wool Textile Manufacturers Federation, Minute Book, 1916–1940, Bradford Archive Office, Bradford Archive Office, File Ref 20D81/6.

Secondary Sources

Allen, G. C. (1970), *British Industries and Their Organisation* (London: Longman, 5th edition).

Barlow, T. D. (1935), 'Surplus capacity in the Lancashire cotton industry', *Manchester School*, Vol. 6.

Bowden, S. and Higgins, D. M. (1998), 'Short-time working and price maintenance: collusive tendencies in the cotton spinning industry, 1919–1939', *Economic History Review*, pp. 319–43.

Bowden, Sue and Higgins, David (1999), 'Productivity on the cheap? The "More Looms" experiment and the Lancashire weaving industry', *Business History*, July, pp. 21–41.

Bowden, S. and Turner, P. (1991), 'Productivity and long term growth potential in the UK economy 1924–1968', *Applied Economics*, Vol. 23, No. 9, pp. 1425–32.

Brearley, A. (1965), *The Woollen Industry*.

Broadberry, S. N. (1983), 'Unemployment in interwar Britain: a disequilibrium approach', *Oxford Economic Papers*, Vol. 35 (Supplement), pp. 463–85.

Broadberry, S. N. (1997), *The Productivity Race; British manufacturing in international perspective, 1850–1990* (Cambridge).

Broadberry, S. N. and Marrison, A., 'External economies of scale in the Lancashire cotton industry, 1900–1939', Paper presented at the Northern Economic History Conference, 10 November 1998.

Bullen, A. J. (1980), The Cotton Spinners and Manufacturers Assoc. and the breakdown of the Collective Bargaining System 1928–35 (Unpublished M.A. thesis, Warwick).

Burnett-Hurst, A. R. (1932), 'Lancashire and the Indian Market', *Journal of the Royal Statistical Society*, Vol. 95.

Chandler, Alfred D. (1990), *Scale and Scope: The Dynamics of Industrial Capitalism*, Cambridge, Mass.

Daniels, G. W. and Jewkes, J. (1928), 'The post-war depression in the Lancashire cotton industry', *Journal of the Royal Statistical Society*, Vol. 91, pp. 153–206.

Dixit, A. and Pindyck, R. (1993), *Investment under Uncertainty* (Princeton: Princeton University Press).

Ellinger, B. and Ellinger H. (1930), 'Japanese competition in the cotton trade', *Journal of the Royal Statistical Society*, Vol. 93, pp. 185–218.

Fowler, A. and Fowler L. (1985), *The History of the Nelson Weavers Association* (Lancashire).

Fowler, A. (1988), 'Lancashire Cotton Trade Unionism in the Inter-War Years', in J. A. Jowitt and A. J. McIvor (eds), *Employers and Labour in the English Textile Industries, 1850–1939*.

Geary, F. (1997), 'The emergence of mass unemployment: wages and employment in shipbuilding between the wars', *Cambridge Journal of Economics*, Vol. 21, pp. 303–21.

Hatton, T. J. (1988), 'A quarterly model of the labour market in interwar Britain', *Oxford Bulletin of Economics and Statistics*, Vol. 50, No. 1 February.

Hatton, Tim (1994), 'Unemployment and the labour market in inter-War Britain', in Roderick Floud and Donald McCloskey (eds), *The Economic History of Britain since 1700*, 2nd edition, Vol. 2 (Cambridge), Ch. 14, pp. 359–85.

Higgins, D. M. and Toms, S. (1997), 'Firm structure and financial performance: the Lancashire textile industry, c. 1884–c. 1960', *Accounting, Business and Financial History*, Vol. 7, pp. 195–232.

Honeyman, K. (1993), 'Montague Burton Ltd: The creators of well dressed men', in J. Chartres and K. Honeyman (eds), *Leeds City Business* (Leeds), pp. 186–216.

Hopwood, E. (1969), *The Lancashire Weavers Story*.

Jowett, J. A. and McIvor, A. J. (eds) (1988), *Employers and Labour in the English Textile Industries, 1859–1939* (London).

Kenny, S. (1982), 'Sub-regional specialisation in the Lancashire cotton industry, 1884–1914: a study in organisational and locational change', *Journal of Historical Geography*, Vol. 8, pp. 41–63.

Lazonick, W. A. (1987), 'The cotton industry' pp. 39–45, in B. Elbaum and W. A. Laxonick (eds) *The Decline of the British Economy* (Oxford: Oxford University Press).

Lucas, Arthur Fletcher (1937) *Industrial Reconstruction and the Control of Competition: The British Experiment* (London: Longman).

McIvor, A. J. (1988), 'Cotton employers' organisations and labour relations, 1890–1939', in J. A. Jowitt and A. J. McIvor (eds), *Employers and Labour in the English Textile Industries, 1850–1939* (London).

McIvor, A. J. (1996), *Organised Capital: Employers' Associations and Industrial Relations in Northern England*, 1880–1939 (Cambridge).

Outram, Quentin (1997), 'The stupidest men in England? The industrial relations strategy of the coal-owners between the lockouts, 1923–1924', *Historical Studies in Industrial Relations*, No. 4 September, pp 65–95.

Rannie, G. F. (ed.) (1965), *The Woollen and Worsted Industry: An Economic Analysis* (Oxford: Clarendon).

Riley, J. H. (1981), The More-Looms System and Industrial Relations in the Lancashire Cotton Manufacturing Industry, 1928–1935, unpublished M.A. thesis (Manchester).

Robson, R. (1957), *The Cotton Industry in Britain* (London: Macmillan).

Sigsworth, E. M. (1990), *Montague Burton: the Tailor of Taste* (Manchester: Manchester University Press).

Thomas, J. (1955), 'A history of the Leeds clothing industry', *Yorkshire Bulletin of Economic and Social Research*, Occasional Paper No. 1.

Turner, Paul and Bowden, Sue (1997), 'Real wages, demand and employment in the UK 1921–1938: a disaggregated analysis', *Bulletin of Economic Research*, Vol. 49, October, pp. 309–25.

Whiteside, Noel (1991), *Bad Times: Unemployment in British Social and Political History* (London).

Whiteside, N. and Gillespie, J. A. (1991), 'Deconstructing unemployment: developments in Britain in the interwar years', *Economic History Review*, Vol. XLIV No. 4, pp. 665–82.

Wood, G. H. (1931), 'Essay on changes in the distribution of British overseas trade in wool textiles during the past ten years', *Weltwirtschaftliches Archiv.* Vol. 33, pp. 503–29.

Wrigley, Chris (1987), *Cosy Co-operation under Strain: Industrial Relations in the Yorkshire Woollen Industry 1919–1939*, University of York Borthwick Paper No. 71, York.

3 The Decline of the UK Textile Industry

The Terminal Years 1945–2003

Allan Ormerod

I. Introduction

It is necessary at the outset to validate that the years 1945–2000 do in fact represent the industry's terminal years. The industry reached its apogee in 1912 with 688,196 employed in spinning, weaving, dyeing, printing and finishing; deployed on 61 million spindles, 786,000 looms and balancing finishing facilities. The industry at that time produced 8.04 billion yards of fabric per year, of which 7.08 billion yards (83%) was exported. Textile manufacturing was industry's major exporter contributing some 25%. The decline in the 1920s and 1930s is well documented by numerous authors.[1] After Bowker's *Seven Terrible Years (1920–27)* the decline continued at a somewhat slower rate until the outbreak of the Second World War, when the industry employed 300,000 and installed capacity had been reduced to 46 million spindles and 340,000 looms, indicative of a 27 year decline in employment, spindles and looms of 57.1%, 25.0% and 56.8%, respectively. The reduction in spinning capacity had been less catastrophic as the spinning sector supplied yarn to the knitting industry which was less exposed to imports, and a substantial spindleage was also employed on the mule spinning of fine Egyptian yarns, which was outside the manufacturing capacity or capability of the developing countries. In 1927 alone, 50 spinning companies, 33 manufacturers, 11 combined spinner/weavers and 79 merchants ceased trading.

This review is restricted to post Second World War from 1945 to 2000. In the year 2000 the industry employed 40,000, 14,000 in each of spinning and weaving, and 12,000 in finishing (source: Office for National Statistics), and its operational equipment had been reduced virtually to zero in cotton and man-made fibre short-staple spinning and 6000 looms in weaving (source: Sulzer Textile Survey). Immediately hostilities ceased in 1945, Government recognised that the only industry capable of increasing activity and exports rapidly was the textile manufacturing industry, and from 1945 until 1952 the industry re-activated cocooned equipment and extended shift working on its most modern machinery, increasing employment from 220,000 to 335,000 by 52%.

Throughout the area of the northwest every advertising site carried the information that 'Britain's Bread Hangs by Lancashire's Thread', associated with an image of a two-pound loaf of bread suspended on a thread of Lancashire-spun yarn. Cinema advertising also included the ubiquitous suspended loaf. Instructions were included on how to proceed in obtaining employment in local factories. Government Ministers, including Sir Stafford Cripps, President of the Board of Trade, and George Isaacs, the Minister of Labour, made several visits to the major textile areas, and the Board of Trade initiated a Working Party under Sir George Schuster and several distinguished independent members. The major object of the investigation was stated to be (1) compulsory amalgamation, (2) schemes to eliminate redundant capacity, and (3) the provision of a re-equipment levy. Between 1946 and 1948 the working party investigation continued, apparently unable to even approach a consensus.

In 1948, however, the Cotton Spinning (Re-equipment Subsidy) Bill was passed, and the Cotton Board Terms of Reference substantially widened and Raymond Streat was appointed as its Chairman. This short-circuiting of the link between the Employer's Association and Government was a major component in the run-down of the industry, and commenced almost immediately the Labour government was replaced by a Conservative administration in 1950 (see Figure 1).

In 1955, during one of my visits to mills in the USA, a leading America textile industrialist and active participant in the American Textile Manufacturers Association described this arrangement as dangerous at best and possibly disastrous; an arrangement which he described as a Trojan Horse. By 1970, with the industry approaching its critical mass with employment and spinning and weaving activity reduced from the 1950 level by 60%, 75% and 69%, respectively, the prediction was fully justified. The Cotton Spinning (Re-equipment Subsidy) Act 1948 was the act that started this massive decline. The precursor of this extraordinary legislation was the Schuster Working Party, the outcome of which could only be described as a shambles. Consisting of fifteen members, including several independents, it was originally set up to review all previous investigations in the industry's affairs prior to making its recommendations. Sir Stafford Cripps, President of the Board of Trade, was responsible for both the

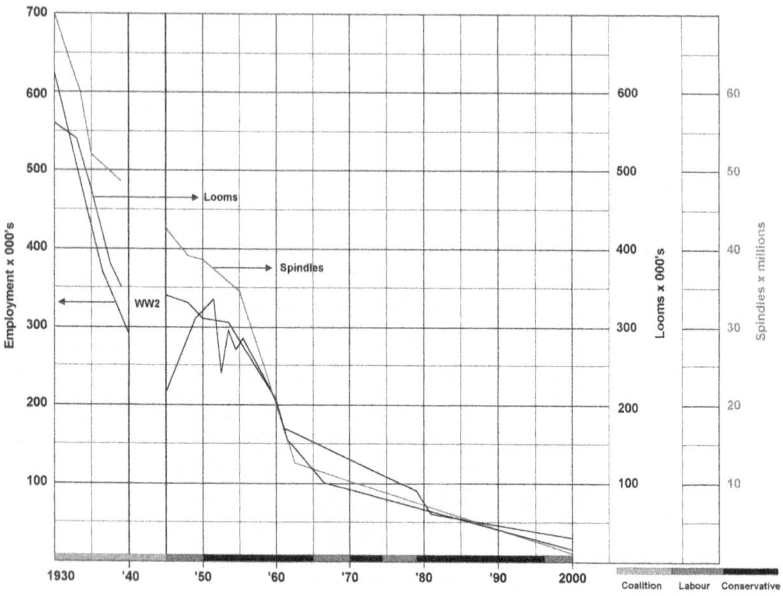

Figure 1 Reduction in Manufacturing Capacity and Employment (1930–2000)

conception and its ultimate outcome. The 234 page report consisted of two halves, the first establishing the industry's problems and the second half setting out 34 recommendations including a scheme to eliminate redundant capacity, a re-equipment levy, and a scheme to improve its basic organisation. Remarkably similar objectives to the 1939 Cotton Enabling Bill that was never implemented as the organisational changes recommended were considered to be incompatible with wartime conditions. The bill was described by Col O. L. Jacks, CBE, MC, the MD of one of the vertical organisations opposing it as 'a device for the unable to disable the able'. The Schuster working party report findings were far from unanimous, all the members objecting to some of the recommendations in a variety of combinations, six of the members objecting to six of the recommendations.[2]

Incredibly the working party was 'passed-on' by the Board of Trade to the re-constituted Cotton Board, the report to be treated as an agenda 'for recommendations to Government for further action', and Sir Raymond Streat was appointed Chairman of the Board with responsibility for its implementation. The Board was also 'to provide a channel through which the industry as a whole would express its views to government'. The Board drafted proposals regarding the controversial recommendations, agreeing with the report on the need for re-equipment, and that large groupings of firms was desirable. A direct grant was proposed in preference to a levy, believing that the grant could be used 'as a carrot to encourage firms to group', and giving priority for the limited supply of textile machinery only to firms of a given size. The report was expected to enable government to determine a new policy for the industry. The new policy, when announced, only remotely related to the report and was concentrated exclusively on the spinning sector! The government would make a grant of 25% towards the cost of new spinning machinery, and if availability was limited, preference was to be given to those firms that chose to participate in the re-organisation proposals, which restricted financial support to mills that re-organised in groups of at least 500,000 spindles. As 500,000 spindles is a large spinning operation, this represents large-scale re-organisation, but the two largest groups already controlled some 70 mills and 40% of the spindles in the spinning sector and both would automatically qualify. Plans for the weaving and finishing sectors and the few vertical organisations were to be postponed 'until the government had fully considered the Evershed committee report on textile machinery and the report of the Chief Inspector of Factories on re-spacing in weaving sheds'. The scheme was never extended.

II. The Cotton Spinning Re-equipment Subsidy 1948

The UK textile industry had been organised horizontally, as this was appropriate for servicing a massive export industry in both yarn and fabric, but was inappropriate both for the application of rapidly changing technology and the change from the predominantly export industry to a domestic industry of increasing complexity and sophistication. Contemporary with publication of the details of the subsidy, the reports of the Anglo-American Productivity Teams became available. The spinning, weaving and finishing teams reported independently on their investigations in American mills. All separately and without collusion identified horizontal organisation as the major impediment to achieving the high productivity of the American mills. The first and most important stage in 'verticalisation' is the combination of spinning and weaving, the final production stage being either acquiring finishing machinery or merging with a finishing organisation equipped and capable of processing the weaving mills' production.

Instead of further extending the already dominant horizontal organisation of the spinning sector, making an even larger cartel than already existed, and complicating yarn procurement for the five hundred horizontally organised weaving mills, the subsidy should have been made available to all mills which combined in spinning-weaving organisations, with a premium for those completing their organisations with a compatible finishing operation. At the time of the working party investigation (1946) the spindles and looms and their associated equipment was distributed as shown in Table 1.

Only 10% of the spindles and 14% of the looms were in either combined spinning-weaving units or fully integrated organisations, including finishing. The subsidy should have been restricted to these units, together with those units that combined into spinning/weaving combinations, with a premium for those which achieved full integration. 'Full integration', as described, relates to production integration; the fully integrated organisation includes sales and marketing, with control from fibre to finished textile.

At the date of the working party investigation there were 165 spinning firms, 744 weaving and 254 finishing firms, or 1163 in total, varying in all three sections over a wide range of capacity.

A professionally qualified and experienced committee could have identified a large number of compatible spinning/weaving linkages and a significant but much smaller and viable fully vertical ones. Ashton Brothers, for example, was used as a hub organisation, a single horizontally organised complex employing 3000 workers changed to a horizontal balanced group by assimilating six substantial spinning, weaving, finishing and marketing companies, increasing the group to a total employment of 6000 and a commensurate addition to

Table 1 Spindles and Looms in Integrated Mills (1946)

Spindles (million)		%
1 In spinning mills	34.1	90
2 In spinning/weaving mills	4.0	10
Total	38.1	100
Looms ('000s)		
1 In weaving mills	350	86
2 In spinning/weaving mills	56	14
Total	406	100

Source: The Cotton Board

Note: The Cotton Board had considered spinning/weaving mills as integrated. However, a small percentage of these were fully integrated, including finishing. About 10,000 of the 56,000 looms were in fully integrated mills in 1949.

turnover. At the time of the Ashton Brothers acquisitions, five years in the mid-1960s, there were a few hundred less firms than when the Schuster committee reported and the 1948 Re-equipment Act was passed, but even in the 1960s there was no difficulty in making these technical and commercial linkages, and the industry would have responded to a suitable carrot. If the last three capacity weaving groups were considered, 26 firms controlled 82,000 looms, which depending on fabrics would normally be balanced by 4 or 5 million spindles. Out of the 165 spinning companies controlling 29.9 million spindles in firms from less than 20,000 spindles to over 1 million, a large possibility for technical and commercials linkages existed for spinning/weaving combination, and a significant number of full verticals by selecting from the 254 finishing firms. A great opportunity was missed of greatly increasing the 10% of the total spindles and

Table 2 Size and Capacity of UK Spinning and Weaving Firms (1939–56)

	Firms		*Million Spindles (m.e.)*	
Spinning Capacity	*1939*	*1956*	*1939*	*1956*
Up to and including 20,000	23	15	0.3	0.2
20,000 to 40,000	38	21	1.0	0.6
40,000 to 60,000	44	23	2.1	1.2
60,000 to 80,000	34	24	2.4	1.7
80,000 to 100,000	34	18	2.2	1.6
100,000 to 200,000	76	34	10.8	4.4
200,000 to 1,000,000	26	25	7.1	8.4
over 1,000,000	5	5	13.2	11.7
Total	280	165	39.1	29.9

	Firms		*Thousand Looms*	
Weaving Capacity	*1939*	*1956*	*1939*	*1956*
Up to and including 200 looms	438	355	38	33
200 to 400	194	141	56	41
400 to 800	253	140	146	82
800 to 2000	153	82	177	96
2000 to 3000	19	16	50	39
3000 to 4000	3	5	10	17
over 4000	3	5	23	26
Total	1063	744	500	333

Note: In 1956 there were 254 firms employing 44,000 operatives in finishing units. Of these 172 or 45% employed less than 100 operatives, and only 20 firms employed more than 400 including 5 employing more than 1000.

14% of the looms that were already in spinning/weaving units, and a substantial number of them, together with the spinning/weaving combination produced by a relevant scheme, could have been converted to full verticals.

In 1958, reasonably adjacent to the date of the Schuster Working Party and the 'government new policy for cotton', a sub-committee of the US Senate published a list of the profit performance of 25 US textile mills arranged in size from the upper to the lower decile. The largest and smallest five are included in Table 3.

The most profitable unit is not included in the first five, and some of the units in the last five are considerably more profitable than some of the units in the first five. The first five were all created by acquisition, as were the largest units in the UK with the exception of Courtaulds Northern Weaving Division (NWD). The last five were built up by internal expansion in new plants, and it is highly probable that there is no economy of scale beyond the size of the firms 21 through 25. Growth by acquisition is very frequently wasteful, and cannot possibly produce the type of tailored operation that is so successful in the

Table 3 Major Textile Interests in the USA Employment and Plants in the Yarn and Fabric Industry

Rank and Interest (ranked in order of magnitude of basic textile employment)	*Basic Textiles (excluding knitting)*				*All Textiles*	
	Employees	*Spindles '000s*	*Looms*	*Plants*	*Plants*	*Employees*
1 Burlington Industries Inc.	45,000	1,362	24,900	78	98	52,500
2 J. & P. Stevens & Co. Inc.	30,500	1,020	25,000	44	44	30,500
3 Cannon Mills Interests	23,200	452	12,325	19	21	24,300
4 Dan River Mills Interests	17,200	821	18,500	17	17	17,200
5 Abney Irvine Interests	16,300	700	15,575	23	23	16,700
21 Callaway Mills	5200	182	2680	6	8	6100
22 Greenwood Mills	5000	292	6860	5	5	5000
23 American Thread Co. Inc.	4500	243	–	7	7	4500
24 Swift and Illges Interests	4500	121	2450	5	5	4500
25 Kendall Co.	4500	322	6990	10	13	5000

Note: Including finishing plants.

USA and in some European countries. Spring Mills are regularly the most profitable textile organisation in the USA by any known index. Springs is a balanced vertical and at the time of the Senate investigation its vital statistics were as follows:

Spinning, weaving, dyeing, printing, garment trades and merchandising: 500 million linear yards of fabric per annum, with a sale value of $200 million and the highest net income per dollar of sales in the industry. Its Grace finishing plant is the largest and most productive in the world, processing 12 million linear yards of fabric per week, almost balancing 18,000 looms and 850,000 spindles.

The Spinning (Re-equipment Subsidy) further propagated the vertical organisation against all technical requirements, whilst the organisation of the most successful textile industries, including USA and Japan, are horizontal. Additionally, it subjected the horizontal weavers (744 companies in existence in 1956) to reduction of price competition in the yarn market by increasing the spinners' control of prices. The 998 firms in the weaving and finishing sectors were excluded from participation. Probably more damaging was the interpolation of the Cotton Board in the industry's negotiating sequence, largely excluding and greatly reducing the effectiveness of the industry's Employers' Association. The government's 'new policy' was strongly advocated by the Chairman, Sir E. Raymond Streat, notwithstanding the fact that it never addressed any of the commercial problems that in the next ten years would necessitate panic legislation to once again address the problem of increasing the now critical penetration of duty-free textiles from the Commonwealth NDCs.

III. The Cotton Industry Act 1959

In March 1960 I became responsible for the affairs of Ashton Brothers and also consequently became actively involved with the Cotton Spinners and Manufacturers Association (CSMA) and Chairman of the Technical Committee of the Association, and my involvement with government departments increased. Throughout 1958 and 1959 we had been obliged to accept a proportion of orders at a loss in order to fully maintain our multi-shift operation and full employment for all our workers. Our capital charges per unit produced (depreciation + interest) were favourable as we had a high level of activity, mainly on modern machinery, so at the expense of a reduced profit situation we were able to maintain full shift activity.

Penetration of the home market by duty-free imported yarn and fabric accelerated, and the export market was in free fall, vulnerable to high tariffs and export markets re-adjusting to balance of payments problems. The industry was endeavouring to survive in the untenable situation of duty-free imports from countries with labour rates that contributed only some 3 or 4% of fabric costs, and fully protected export markets. Factories closed down at the rate of three or four per week, and many of the survivors were unable to maintain balanced activity as workers left for more secure employment. Although it was obvious that unless some action was taken to control duty-free imports from Commonwealth countries, particularly India, Pakistan and Hong Kong (currently 35%), the industry would be eliminated. No acknowledgement was either made in the Act or in indications in discussion with the Board of Trade, that over 220,000 jobs were at risk and a massive import bill inevitable.

The assistance provided by the Act was to make funds available for eliminating excessive capacity in all three sectors, spinning, weaving and finishing, and provide financial assistance for re-equipment for the companies that decided to take advantage of the scheme. The owners of the scrapped equipment were to be compensated at a prescribed rate, with a premium rate for mills that ceased to manufacture. The Treasury commitment depended on the number of installed spindles and looms that were scrapped, but those who remained in business were to provide one-third of the total cost of scrapping. The word 'installed' was clearly intended by the originators of the scheme in Whitehall to restrict payment to machinery that had been in recent operation. 'Installed' was interpreted in the industry to mean bolted to the floor with access to a power source, and a large proportion of machinery qualified for payment that was obsolete and should have been scrapped before the Second World War. The sound companies, with little or nothing to scrap were obliged to pay one third of the scrapping bill and made efficient firms less competitive. The re-equipment grant for approved projects provided 25% of the cost of new machinery. The qualifying clause was not particularly onerous, but when the 25% was considered in relation to related depreciation accounting it was reduced to 12½%. As foreign textile machinery, particularly Swiss, German and Italian, was more technically advanced than the UK machinery which had a massive market in the NDCs, the progressive mills purchased overseas and paid 20% import duty if a 'similar' machine was manufactured in the UK. As a machine with a 50% higher production rate and requiring only 60% of the labour required for equivalent output, if it could 'make the product', it was assessed as similar. In modern mills the machinery cost more under the scheme than purchased independently, as the scrapping element was obligatory.

Consistent with previous government legislation to assist the industry, the vertical sector that should have been given maximum assistance was penalised. Most of these mills were well equipped with ring spindles, automatic looms and balanced finishing capacity, and with no spinning mules or non-automatic looms to scrap, had nothing to register for scrapping compensation. Nevertheless, they had to make substantial contributions to the owners of this industrial archaeology. They were also obliged to contribute to scrapping in the horizontally organised finishing sector, even though precluded from taking advantage of the scheme for any obsolete plant, as scrapping in the finishing sector was for some inexplicable reason restricted to companies closing down complete finishing plants. Thus, a completely vertical organisation was obliged to pay levies to scrap equipment in the horizontal finishing sector, diverting capital from selective developments in the vertical sector. Significant capital intended for further development of vertical organisations was paid out to owners of the spinning mules and non-automatic looms that should have been scrapped after the First World War. As my Chairman, Col O. L. Jacks, CBE, MC, remarked at the time 'the cash which we intended to use for increasing our shuttle-less weaving capacity has probably financed retirement villas in Lytham and Southport'.

It was argued by the originators and advocates of the scheme that vertical units would obtain 'indeterminate but nevertheless substantial benefits by future trading in an industry with less productive capacity'. I never believed this even in 1959, and the mill closures associated with duty-free imports – which ceased immediately the government scrapping scheme was announced – would, if continued at the then existing rate, have reduced the industry to its 1963 size without external intervention and artificial stimulus. Of the 12.44 million spindles and 104,747 looms scrapped under the scheme, 72% of the spindles and 74% of the looms were idle and unstaffed and of no competitive significance. The equipment that remained is also interesting. At the end of 1961, 9.01 million spindles were in production, of which 5.98 were ring spindles, 2.36 mule and 0.67 condenser waste. Of the 141,000 looms in production, 94,000 were non-automatic and 47,000 automatic. Thus, there were still more mule spindles and non-automatic looms in the UK industry after scrapping than in the rest of Europe, indicating that 27% of the spinning machinery and 66% of the weaving machinery was still obsolete. In a paper presented to the Annual Meeting of the British Association of the Advancement of Science in 1962,[3] an organisation and staffing to produce 2,000 million square yards of the fabric in the constructions in production at that time would require 95,000 looms and 5.40 million spindles on two shifts; but on three shifts, which were essential for the equipment currently available, the production could be achieved on 3.6 million spindles and 63,000 looms. The trade organisation to implement this policy is shown in Table 4.

Table 4 was based on a realistic intermediate conversion stage in moving from a 90% horizontal situation existing in 1959 to an organisation based on the situation in the notes to the table. The scrapping scheme had little or no effect on the industry's organisation.

Although the ratio of looms associated with spindles increased, this was almost exclusively the result of scrapping 12.4 million spindles and 104,747 looms. Neither was the scheme the catalyst for efficiency that its sponsors expected. The huge recorded increase in production per unit of installed capacity followed inevitably from eliminating the

Table 4 Trade Organisation to Produce and Market an Annual Requirement of 2000 million square yards of Fabric

	Distribution of Capacity			
Activity	*Fully Integrated Verticals*	*Combined Spinner/Weaver*	*Horizontal Sectional*	*Total Trade Capacity*
Merchanting % value	63	–	37	100
Finishing % Capacity	40	–	60	100
Weaving Capacity Looms	43,000	15,000	37,000	95,000
Spinning Capacity Spindles	2,000,000	900,000	2,500,000	5,400,000
Ratio Spindles/ Looms	46.5	60.0	67.8	57.0
Ratio Looms to units of Finishing capacity	1070	–	865	–

Note: (1) Horizontal finishers working for both horizontal weavers and combined spinner/weavers.
(2) Figures based on distribution of fabrics between cloth constructions existing in 1957–58.
(3) Weaving organisation based on an average of 0.172 loom hours/sq. yd. This compares with 0.192 loom hours/sq. yd currently being achieved. The difference is due to selective application of shuttle-less weaving machines and high-speed conventional automatic looms.
(4) Two shift working on all machinery.

huge quantity of obsolete and inactive equipment from the calculation. The real increase in productivity from October 1958 up to the end of 1961 was 16% for spinning and 9% for weaving; which considering that the 1958 figures were affected by extensive short-time working was an unsatisfactory result. Appendix C in the Fourth Report of the Estimates Committee shows the change in productivity in spinning and weaving in the three years covering the implementation of the scrapping and re-equipment scheme.

Consistent with every scheme in which the government had a major influence, elimination of capacity and/or expansion of horizontal organisation were the major objectives, and re-equipment very much a secondary consideration. That this was the situation in relation to the 1959 Act was clearly stated in Section 265 of the Report of the Fourth Estimates Committee.

During discussion of the Re-organisation Scheme, it was stated by the senior representative of the Board of Trade: 'It (the re-equipment scheme) was always a second and perhaps lesser, but still an important section of the Act.'

During the next five years duty-free imports and global quotas both increased at a massive rate. From 35% market penetration in 1959, the date of the Act, this increased to 56% throughout 1966 and to 77% during the first quarter of 1967, the increase predominantly duty-free. Highly capital-intensive equipment purchased under the Act and which required three-shift activity for profitability was running double or single shifts within two years of installation. The industry had invested £23.418 million in the scheme, inclusive of the contribution for scrapping, believing that duty-free access would at least be restricted to the 1959 level, leaving market growth for the domestic industry. Government expenditure on scrapping and re-equipment was £23 million, and when considered from any perspective a combined expenditure of £56.418 million produced a deplorable return on investment. The huge investment was made on scrapping machinery, a very high proportion of which had not produced for years and would never have produced again. Had the scheme been restricted to machines producing at the date the scheme was announced, the scrapping contribution from the mills with little or nothing to scrap would have been greatly reduced. The industry contributed £6 million to dispose of this industrial archaeology. Figure 1 shows that at the time of implementation of the Act, i.e. 1959–62, the imports were increasing at 2.7% of the market per year or in excess of 8%, destroying the declared intensions of the Act! Some of the equipment was never removed from packing cases and shipped overseas several years after delivery to the mills, and new high-tech equipment ceased to recover depreciation and interest within two years of installation. In a discussion with Anthony Burney (later Sir Anthony), the chosen administrator of the scheme, on the occasion of his visit to Ashton Brothers during a tour of selected mills to obtain 'trade-reaction' to the provisions of the Act, I predicted that the rate of attrition at the date of the Act would reduce the industry to the size the government expected to achieve within five years if no action was taken. I also told him that unless government restricted duty-free imports to their existing level the industry could not survive, as our most modern mill still included a 27% labour element, compared with the 3 or 4% in Commonwealth imports. I explained that although technology was rapidly reducing the labour content of yarn and fabric it would take many years to discount the present difference of some 23%, and that at the current rate of attrition the industry would not survive long enough to take advantage of the situation. The situation was reached in 2000 when the industry was reduced to 40,000 workers and still reducing at a steady rate of 8000 per year (source: Office for National Statistics, 1998–2000). Figure 2, maximum weft insertion rate (1900–1996), clearly demonstrates that effective competition in the weaving sector only became possible in the 1990s; a similar if somewhat less spectacular situation existing with spinning delivery speeds.

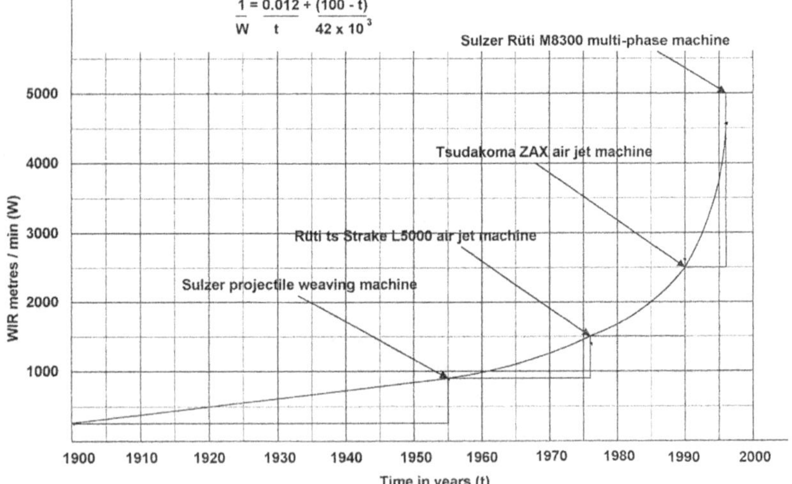

Figure 2 Maximum Weft Insertion Rate (1900–1996)

IV. The Textile Council Report. 'Cotton and Allied Textiles', Vol. 1 and 2 (1969)

In the ten years since participating in the Cotton Industry Act (1959), market penetration had increased by a further 16% to 51%, the UK industry now a minority supplier to the UK market. In response to the industry's request that further duty-free imports should not be authorised, the Permanent Secretary of the Board of Trade proposed that the Textile Council should undertake a study 'of the ways which the efficiency and productivity of the industry could be rapidly increased'. This requirement was proof that the Board of Trade had no knowledge of either the magnitude of the various cost elements in fabric as manufactured in India and Europe, or the magnitude of possible reduction in labour unit cost per m^2 of fabric even if capital was available to install the most productive spinning and weaving machinery then available. Our investigations confirmed that an association of UK labour cost and the most capital-intensive machines could reduce the labour unit cost per m^2 of fabric to between 22 and 24%, depending on the construction of the particular fabric. The technology to achieve parity with Indian labour costs was guesstimated at 25 years ahead, and our major objective was trying to survive for the next twelve months! Throughout all the post-war negotiations with the Board of Trade, they continually failed to understand, or acknowledge the magnitude of the difference in cost per m^2 resulting directly from difference in hourly wage costs, or the rate of change of reduction of that difference made possible by technology and machinery development. Adventitiously, the inability to compete irrespective of capital intensity, productivity, efficiency and activity was conclusively proved by the Courtaulds Northern Weaving Division (NSD) new mills project. The NWD programme in 1970 was to manufacture 124 million m^2 per annum in the Skelmersdale plant, 56 million m^2 in the two new plants at Carlisle and Lillyhall, and 40 million m^2 in total from the automatic loom mills and non-automatic loom mills in Lancashire, acquired in recent acquisitions. Subsequent to my association with Courtaulds NWD, four additional new high-tech weaving mills were added and the Carlisle and Lillyhall plants were substantially extended. With an estimated total production potential of 320 million m^2, or approximately 40% of the residual UK market, this was a massive act of faith.

To demonstrate the limitation of technology in increasing productivity and reducing unit labour cost, a description of the Skelmersdale plant is relevant. This was the largest and most capital intensive weaving operation constructed in the west since the First World War, built on a 20 acre site with 644,296ft^2 of buildings with a circumscribing rectangle of 1231ft × 520ft, accommodating 836 Ruti Model C looms and 644 Kovo air jet shuttle-less weaving machines with the most productive preparation machinery. The factory generated its own power from Mirlees Diesel engine-driven Bush alternators, each of 2.35 MVA providing current at 11,000V transformed in three sub-stations to 415V. Investment in buildings and plant was £9.6 million, inclusive of £3.68 million government grant. The mill was designed to consume 870,000 lbs of yarn per week from the Company's mills in Northern Spinning Division (NSD), a production adequate to support seven or eight multi-shift spinning mills. Over £13 million was invested including working capital providing for 1100 workers organised on a 4 shift 168 hour week. The mill, when worked up to standard efficiency, was never able to compete with import prices by a substantial margin, proving that the most advanced technology had still a long way to go before the labour cost difference per m^2 could be discounted.

With the Courtauld experience allied with new mill cost experience in Ashton Brothers, it was clear that the higher productivity and efficiency investigation that the Board of Trade required could never produce a total cost convergence of a magnitude even approaching total cost parity with duty-free imports from Commonwealth NDCs. For this reason I thought long and hard before accepting the Chairman's invitation to join both the Executive and Editing Committees with responsibility for producing the Textile Council report. During my association with the industry, Government had been actively involved with three investigations, none of which addressed the industry's problems. They had been technically naive, lacking in investigative rigour, and in many cases reached conclusions unjustified by the inadequate analysis. This invitation at least provided the opportunity to structure a fully comprehensive study, with conclusions and recommendations based on the results of sound analysis of established facts. The report entitled 'Cotton and Allied Textiles' Volumes 1 and 2 – a report on present performance and future prospects, with 299 pages including 100 pages of statistics – was recognised at the time to be the most comprehensive and authoritative study of any textile industry. Every aspect was considered, including organisation, exploitable technology and technical progress, analysis of international production costs and profitability, investigation of the economic effects of various systems of shift working and order quantity, product and market rationalisation, and a study of the factors determining profitability in the three process sectors, spinning, weaving and finishing. All the constraints retarding progress were comprehensively studied and appropriate recommendations made.

In the introduction to the report, Sir James Steel, the Chairman of Council, set out a list of what government must be prepared to do if the industry was to carry through the recommended programme of root and branch re-organisation and re-equipment capable of achieving maximum possible labour cost convergence with the landed costs of duty-free products from the NDCs.

These were:

1 Introduce a tariff on Commonwealth imported cotton textiles.
2 Prevent a destructive rise in imports during the period in which the industry is adjusting to reliance on tariff protection alone.
3 Swift and more effective action to avoid dumping and other malpractices which result in distortion of trade.
4 Government should encourage re-equipment in the traditional textile areas by giving the incentives of investment grants no less favourable than those available in development areas.

If the government had carried out their obligations as set out in the report as a mandatory requirement, the programme as outlined was capable of moving the industry into line with the most competitive industries in Europe. In the Executive Committee we emphasised to the Board of Trade assessor that if this stability was either not provided or inadequate, there would inevitably be a repeat of the inadequate response to the re-equipment phase of the 1959 Act. One member of the Editing Committee, Mr E. T. Gartside, tabled a Note of Dissent that was included in the report. He considered that the obligations of government as set out in the report were inadequate, and that UK market penetration should not exceed that of other European textile industries. This was a perfectly legitimate observation, but five of us on the Executive Committee had been involved with Ministers in Whitehall and involved in unproductive arguments with Board of Trade officials, and we believed that if we could draw a line at the then current capacity of 10.1 million spindles and 125,000 looms with a labour force of 105,000, and re-organise and re-equip in conformity with the findings of the report, we could service domestic expansion by re-equipment and activity increased by more shift working; hopefully now represented by a less compliant organisation with no direct association with or responsibility to the government, the situation which existed with the Cotton Board. The US and European textile organisations negotiated directly and permanently with their Governments and maintained permanent well-staffed organisations in headquarters adjacent to Government.

The Chairman's caveat was ignored, and unrestricted imports of fabric from India, Pakistan and Hong Kong continued. To make investments of a magnitude to satisfy the programme outlined in the Textile Council Report with no prospects of permanent control of duty-free imports would have been financially irresponsible and there was insignificant response, with the exception of Courtaulds new mills project in NWD. As explained in section 4 the most sophisticated weaving operation certainly in Europe was unable to discount the hourly labour cost difference between the UK and the NDCs. NWD was conceived as a conduit for connecting spun viscose yarn from Courtaulds fibre plants via Northern Spinning Division (NSD). The chemicals to finished fabric integration would have been moderately profitable with even modest duty protection, but none was forthcoming. From both the horizontal and vertical sections of the Lancashire industry there was no response. The industry was being sacrificed to a government policy of Commonwealth preference. In a meeting in 1958 between officers of the Cotton Board and the Board of Trade, an official from the Colonial Office was present, Sir Arthur Hylton Poynton. During the discussion he referred indignantly to 'this cosseted welfare-state industry ... should keep these poor people from earning a crust of bread or a bowl of rice'.[4]

At the time market penetration was 35% predominantly duty free, and in the next ten years it increased by 88% to 66%, the increase linear with time as shown in Figure 1. During this period the Cotton Board and Board of Trade agreed not to stop the trade but prevent it from reaching unmanageable proportions. However, a significant section of the industry considered that drawing the line at the 1962 level of market penetration was unacceptable, and that a substantial reduction was the minimum requirement. The following quotation is from the Epilogue in Sir Raymond Streat's Diary. 'This provoked the antagonism of the smaller companies who felt that the Council (The Textile Council) was a tool of government rather than a body representing the views of the industry', an accusation formerly directed at the Cotton Board, based on much more convincing evidence. The Textile Council Report, 'Cotton and Allied Textiles', was the only report presented by industry to government that supported assistance and survival of the efficient upper quartile of the industry, as opposed to appeasing the most articulate lower quartile at the expense of the former. The report, even when read in 2003, is still largely relevant and technically and commercially sound when related to an industry which was still not beyond the critical mass stage and still possessed adequate capacity in all three sectors. It should be studied by all members of the TCSG, and all those responsible for the new strategy for the textile manufacturing industry.

V. The Textile and Clothing Strategy Group (TCSG). Report and Government Response

The Department of Trade and Industry (DTI) provided the initiative for a new industrial strategy, associating textile manufacturing and clothing as a single industry. The clothing industry had made a substantial contribution to the unlimited access to duty-free fabric from the Commonwealth countries. The attraction of low cost loom-state fabric, which could be finished in the UK in the horizontal finishing sector which was eagerly seeking replacement fabric for that formerly provided by the weaving sector of the UK textile manufacturing industry, appeared too good to miss. The difference in cost of loom state fabric made it possible to manufacture clothing relatively inefficiently and still undercut the legitimate European competition, which did not have the unique availability of duty-free fabric from NDCs. However, this huge advantage was dissipated over time, until a point was reached at which the garment and fabric retailers, led by Marks & Spencer, decided to import manufactured garments from the NDCs, in preference to loom state fabric. The DTI was faced with a situation of elimination of the clothing industry and the textile finishing industry. No single clothing industry exists worldwide in a country which does not possess a substantial textile manufacturing industry, and there was insufficient spinning and weaving capacity available capable of making a realistic contribution to the missing loom state fabric.

After fifty years of continuously increasing imports, market penetration exceeded 90%, and textile import value had reached £15.41 billion (TCSG report) and added value had been reduced to £6.46 billion. Unless the textile manufacturing industry could be at least partially re-activated and a significant part of the clothing industry saved, the prospect of adding the £6.41 billion added value to the already ludicrous £15.41 billion imports, resulting in an early importation of £21.87 billion, was a sickening possibility.

This provided the rationale for considering the two industries as one, and evolving a strategy to at least retain the estimated 180,000 workers still involved in the two industries.

To consider the two industries as one, and endeavour to provide a common strategy, was never a realistic possibility. The textile industry in 2000 was in the upper decile of capital intensity bracketed with petroleum products at £170,000 per worker, and the clothing industry was in the bottom decile bracketed with leather goods and furniture. Even a textile spinning and weaving plant of modest size currently costs between £20 and 30 million, compared with a few hundred thousand for a stitching operation. For textile manufacturing multi-shift organisation is essential and 6000 hours per year is mandatory, whereas single shift operation is economical for stitching operations. Furthermore, relations between the two activities could hardly be described as cordial, for obvious reasons. The most successful Western textile industries, USA, Italy, and Switzerland had retained large textile manufacturing industries with clothing manufacture integrated for many products, moving stitching operations for run-of-the-mill qualities into low wage economies (US to Mexico and the Caribbean, Italy to North Africa and Switzerland to Portugal). The raison d'etre for creating the TCSG was also bordering on the bizarre. The declared objective was to prevent the textile manufacturing and clothing industries from declining to their critical mass. The situation in textile manufacturing in 2000 was as shown in Figure 1. The spinning section of the industry was approaching extinction and the small weaving capacity was reduced to 6000 looms and the much contracted knitting capacity existed almost exclusively on yarn imported from the Commonwealth. A few years ago the UK textile manufacturing industry ceased to be included in many international textile statistics, the decision having been taken that a few hundred looms existing exclusively on imported yarn and a finishing sector organised almost exclusively on the further processing of imported fabric does not constitute a textile manufacturing industry. Critical mass in textile manufacturing is reached when a combination of balanced facilities in all three sections is only just capable of manufacturing a limited range of basic textiles and to maintain continuity of an economical shift pattern. This position was reached several years ago when 2.5 million spindles and 30,000 looms were fully operational with balanced finishing capacity. With this capacity a recovery situation and a basis for expansion still existed.

In 2003 the group reviewed its progress in a report 'Making it Happen'. Although the TCSG report included statistics, presumably to establish the status quo as a basis against which to measure future progress, the progress report was devoid of any comparative figures against which to measure either progress or regression resulting from three years application of the 'National Strategy'. Several relevant figures had been provided in the TCSG report against which some comparative figures are essential. These included annual textile import value, related domestic added value, employment in textile manufacturing, spinning, weaving and finishing, and investment per worker per year during the three years during which the strategy had been implemented. Neither capital investment nor an appreciation of the significance of the textile machinery revolution, were considered in the report, but the cost of the omission of both is unforgivable. The textile machinery revolution, clearly demonstrated in Figures 2 and 3, was never even recognised.

In the absence of comparative statistics in the progress report, which can only be considered as a disturbing omission, an effort has been made to provide some indication of progress or recession. Factory closures in all manufacturing sectors and clothing plants have been both regular and at a disturbing frequency. The employment in textile manufacturing and finishing were incorrectly stated in the TCSG

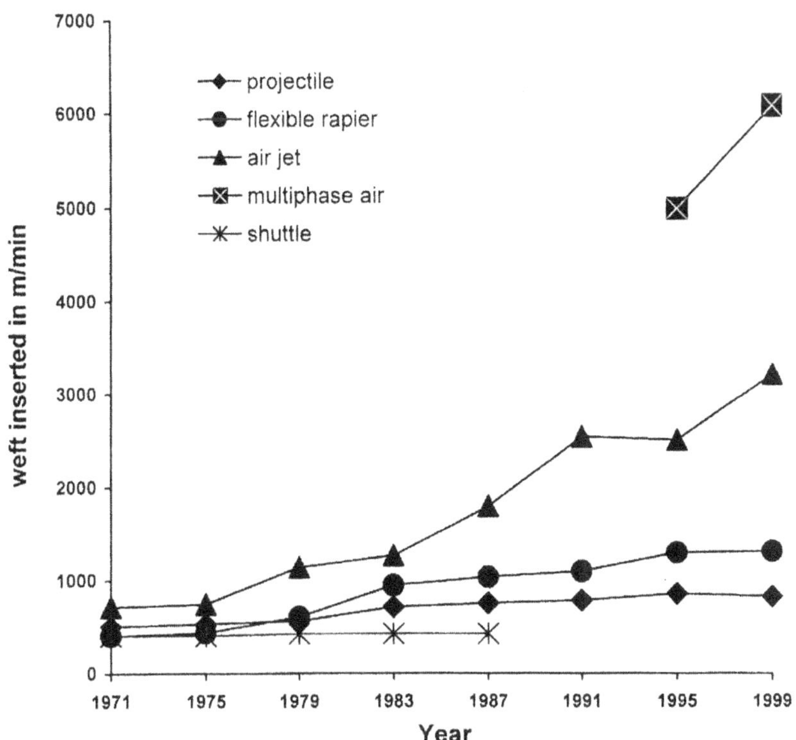

Figure 3 Maximum Weft Insertion Rates of 190cm Wide Weaving Machines at ITMAs 1971–99

report to be 130,000 and 19,000 respectively. This was clearly incorrect as short-staple cotton and man-made fibre spinning was virtually non-existent and looms down to 6000 (Sulzer Survey). The figures for 2000 provided by the DTI, sourced from the Office for National Statistics, were 14,000, 14,000, and 12,000, respectively, for spinning, weaving, and finishing, having fallen by 16,000 in total since 1998.

To obtain some indication of the situation I abstracted ten months mill and installed equipment sales in the appropriate section of *Textile Month*. Although this will not include all plant closures the most significant will be included. In ten months between August 2001 and June 2002, 20 substantial textile plants offered their premises and/or manufacturing facilities for sale. These included some very substantial well-equipped mills, such as Swan Lane, Bolton (cotton and synthetic spinning), Strines Textiles, Stockport (printing, dyeing and finishing), Firth Carpets, Fruit of the Loom, Campsie (spinning, shuttle-less weaving and circular knitting with balanced dyeing and finishing machinery). The total employment of the 20 plants is difficult to quantify, but 200 per plant would be a conservative estimate, aggregating 4000 workers. Extrapolating for the three years of TCSG mandate would indicate a probable 14,400; reducing the 40,000 in the Office for National Statistics 2000 figures to 25,600 at the end of 2003. This indicates that the rate of reduction in employment established by the Office for National Statistics between 1998 and 2000, i.e. the two years before TCSG's watch, has not been reduced, much less reversed.

The percentage added value of a typical textile manufacturing industry will vary from 65 to 70%, varying with product complexity. The following figures are provided in the TCSG report for the 2000 situation.

Turnover	(£ billion)	21.94
Imports		15.41
Added value		6.46
Percentage added value		29.40

The figures for 2003 will be considerably worse, as imports have increased substantially to replace the production of the rapidly shrinking capacity. Imports could be up to the £17.5 billion and added value reduced to £4.4 billion on a textile turnover of almost £22 billion. No comparable figures were provided in the progress report 'Making it Happen'. It would have been surprising if the predicted favourable outcome had been achieved, as the 55 recommendations in the report were largely peripheral and unrelated to the textile manufacturing industry's problems. The detritus which remains has no possibility of competing effectively with imports from the upper quartile European mills, much less the NDC's. The whole subject of investment and capital development was dismissed in 134 words in a report of 44 pages. This would have been indefensible at any time between 1950 and 1990, but for the Group to be unaware of the textile machinery revolution in spinning and weaving between 1990 and 2000 is incredible. Weft insertion rates in weaving increased in eight years in two steps from 1500 to 5500 metres per minute. Spinning speeds have now increased to over 150,000 tpm in open-end spinning and 300,000 in Vortex air jet spinning.

In January 2001 Patricia Hewitt MP, the Minister of State at the DTI, stated in correspondence:

> Low labour costs in newly developed countries will always pose a threat to textile manufacturing as UK companies cannot compete at this level.

In November 1997 Mr John Battle MP, the Minister of State for Science, Energy and Industry, had responded to the submission of a fully developed feasibility study to establish a combined spinning and weaving plant with 1997 technology demonstrating profitable manufacture in competition with duty-free import prices from NDCs.

> Attractive though the proposals may seem ... I am afraid that they are unlikely to prove practicable. It is inherently unlikely that the UK's lost mainstream capacity in mature industries such as these (textile manufacturing and textile machinery manufacture) which face intensive competition, can be regenerated as suggested.

Not a single reason for this observation was produced, or a single observation on the fully detailed feasibility study. Comparative hourly wage costs dominate the Department's thinking, notwithstanding the fact that UK textile wages are the lowest in Western Europe with the exception of Portugal, being 45% less than the highest and 14% less than Italian wages in a highly profitable textile manufacturing industry which is the second largest exporter of textiles in the world ($17.17 billion per year). The dominant effect of low hourly wage rates started to change in the late 1980s, which is fully explained by Figures 2 and 3 and Table 5.

If trans-oceanic transport and entry and freight charges are added to the ex-works of the NDCs, it is doubtful if 3 or 4% landed cost difference would compensate for the additional costs of doing business

Table 5 Comparative Costs of Fabric Production in Vertical Spinning and Weaving Factories 1997 (ITMF)

Producing Country	*Total Cost per linear yd × 66 inches wide ($)*	*% of Total Cost of Labour*	*Comparative Costs USA Factory (USA=100)*
Brazil	0.923	0.102 (11%)	101.2
Korea	0.917	0.129 (14%)	100.5
Turkey	0.891	0.031 (3%)	92.7
Indonesia	0.836	0.012 (2%)	91.7
USA	0.912	0.185 (20%)	100.0

in the NDCs.[5] Even before the revolutionary machinery became available, factories in the west equipped with 1995 technology were capable of achieving the landed cost of most NDCs on an identical spun and woven product. The US mill in Table 5 achieved this dominance without either the Tsudakoma ZAX or the Sulzer multi-phase air-jet weaving machine, but were using Sulzer 1995 projectile weaving machines. The US costs still included 20% labour content, which could be reduced to 10% by using 2000 technology equipment, with a dramatic effect on total cost.

The massive effect of technological developments was amplified by rapidly increasing hourly wage rates in many NDCs. For example, labour costs in South Korea were increased by 300% between 1991 and 2002, the associated labour costs in manufacturing increasing from 6 to 12%.[6] The total manufacturing costs of the South Korea mills did not increase during this period of rapidly increasing hourly rates. Brazilian textile hourly wages also increased by about 60% of the rate during the same period, and the remaining NDCs will inevitably follow. The major characteristic of textile manufacturing costs in the last ten years has been the reduction in labour costs by more than financial costs (depreciation plus interest) necessary to achieve them. This applies particularly to the mills in the USA, Germany and France that have invested in 2000 technology. In spite of all the evidence, the DTI still believe that hourly wage rates are decisive.

Since the 1939 Cotton Industry Enabling Bill, the textile manufacturing industry has been subjected to several investigations, none of which – with the exception of the Textile Council Report, 'Cotton and Allied Textiles' – has addressed the industry's basic problems: but the report of the Textile and the Clothing Strategy Group has failed even to identify the problem. The DTI claim to have expended £75 million in the textile manufacturing industry in the last four or five years, and

£15 million has been made available for the TCSG. No publication of the return on this £90 million investment has been produced. Statistics of employment, production, mill closures, or capital investment in manufacturing organisations do not provide any indication that the 55 strategic recommendations have even retarded the rate of closure or activated the commissioning of new plants. As will be demonstrated later, the £90 million would have financed four such plants in new buildings or £77.8 million in existing buildings, producing £64 million of annual income from four modest installations, and making a significant reduction in the £15.4 billion (and increasing) import bill.

VI. Personal Involvement with the Board of Trade and Department of Trade and Industry

During the period 1955 to 1970 I had an on-going involvement with the Board of Trade in my capacity sequentially as director and production manager, general manager and managing director, and group managing director of the Ashton Group, and as Chairman of the Technical Committee of the Cotton Spinners and Manufacturers Association. My first experience relating to a capital development was associated with the manufacture of a 300 thread per square inch poplin that we manufactured for export to the bespoke shirt maker Hathaway in the USA. With only one other manufacturer world-wide manufacturing the fabric and only two spinners producing 2/160 combed Sea Island cotton yarn from which the fabric was produced, this was an important export business for this and associated poplin export qualities. In the Ashton mills we had the largest installation of automatic looms in the UK, and as some 2000 out of a total of 2400 were manufactured by the British Northrop Loom Company it was logical to procure from the same source. A further hundred machines were required, an order of some significance to any loom manufacturer, and there was little difficulty in negotiating a satisfactory technical specification and price. However, the MD of Northrop attended the negotiation, and objected to a very reasonable request not to include a metal stand and box for accommodating the weft yarn. We had designed a machine for automatically sorting the cleaned weft bobbins off a battery of Terrel stripping machines, and counting and delivering a predetermined number with all the locating rings at the same side of the box to facilitate filling of the automatic loom batteries. As the looms were for installation in an existing plant in which this equipment was located, it was essential that we had the box and stand of our own design and manufacture. However, he was prepared to leave them off the machines but not to make an appropriate discount to the cost! As we were Northrop's largest customer worldwide this was unacceptable and I refused to accept the MD's condition. As he knew that my alternative was foreign-built machines with 20% import duty he did not believe that I had an alternative, and was the most surprised man in the country when he lost the order.

On returning to consider the alternative source, my Chairman showed me a recent cutting from the *Manchester Guardian* reporting that the Sulzer Company in Switzerland had installed 96 shuttle-less weaving machines in a mill in Alsace. I knew that they were developing a shuttle-less machine based on the Rossman patents, but was unaware that it had reached commercial acceptance. I visited Sulzer and spent a couple of days in the research and development departments, prior to visiting the mill in Alsace with the Sales Director. After a full day on the relatively short performance history and examining fabric both loom state and finished, I returned to Zurich and ordered 24 machines at £3000 fob per machine, subject to Board confirmation. The 24 machines were capable of producing the same output as the 100 automatic looms from the British Northrop Loom Company, although paying approximately 60% more for the production capacity required there were large manufacturing cost savings in down-stream warp and weft preparation, in weaving and maintenance cost, and reduced reject fabric.

As Chairman of the technical committee of the CSMA, I was familiar with the legislation relating to the duty free importation of foreign textile machinery, which made duty free qualification dependant on 'comparability'. If a comparable machine existed in the UK neither price nor other criteria was relevant. If the machines were to attract duty a further £14,410 would be required to finance the project. 'Comparability' would have to be extrapolated into an area of fantasy if a machine costing six times the price, or three times as productive depending on the product, 60% less labour intensive, with a quality capability impossible to achieve on shuttle looms, maintenance costs relative to shuttle looms established both in Sulzer and the Alsace plant of less than a third, and great ergonomic and reduced noise advantages hitherto impossible to achieve in weaving. How could such a revolutionary machine be comparable to a shuttle loom based on Northrop 1898 patents? A duty free licence was applied for, supported by a full technical and economic evaluation. The application was rejected. The file rapidly increased in thickness over the next few weeks as the civil-servants in the Board of Trade invited opinions from the British Cotton Industry Research Association, UK loom manufacturers, including British Northrop, and UK textile manufacturers who had recently installed Northrop looms.

As it was our intention to duplicate the first order in future capital development programmes, £145,000 would be involved, a sizeable investment equivalent to over £4 million in 2000. I applied for and was granted an interview at the Board of Trade (BOT). Although it was clear from the correspondence that the case for establishing 'comparability' was indefensible, we prepared a complete and numerate justification for the machine complete with comparative manufacturing costing, fabric samples, calculations of saving in building costs and air conditioning equipment and associated power costs of changing from shuttle looms to Sulzer projectile shuttle-less weaving machines.[7] I concluded the presentation by pointing out that the Board were not doing British Northrop any favours by protecting the manufacturer of a machine which had changed little in basic design since Ashton Brothers purchased the first automatic looms from Draper Corporation in the USA in 1903, before they were manufactured in the UK, and that their best interests would be served by exposing them to competition to stimulate development. Twenty years later, the British Northrop Loom Company, then the largest loom maker in Europe, had ceased to exist. I had prepared to be interrogated by at least one engineer and technologist, as such decisions were not within the capacity of administrators and economists. However, it was becoming increasingly difficult for the BOT to write letters on this issue that made any sense, and a few weeks later we received a letter including a licence to import the machines duty free, which established the case for the remainder of the textile industry.

The next Ashton v Board of Trade encounter (1962) relates to the importation of a continuous bleaching range from Germany. Although we finished towels and related products in the Ashton complex, we had our sheeting products bleached, dyed and finished by commission finishers, who operated a minimum price scheme administered by their trade association. The fabric was processed in a discontinuous pressure kier that had several technical disadvantages and one commercial disadvantage, in that it was prohibitively expensive to operate. The cost of the kier process was 9.4 old pence per pound, compared with 3.0 old pence for the combined hydrogen peroxide/sodium hypo-chlorite process in continuous J boxes. No UK textile engineer manufactured a continuous bleaching range. The associated equipment, predominately finishing stenter and finishing chasing-calender was manufactured by Mather and Platt and could be purchased economically from a UK supplier. The whole installation to process 70,000 pounds weight of sheeting per week required a completely new plant in substantial new buildings.[8] The financial analysis was made on the recently accepted DCF (IRR) as an index of financial acceptability, but calculated on this basis the IRR was 35.7% and the NPV (net present value) £327,000 or 1.63 times the initial investment. The plant was opened in March 1963, by the MP for the Stalybridge and Hyde constituency, Mr Fred Blackburn, who had expended considerable time and effort to influence his colleagues in Government with respect to our various applications for relaxation of duty on foreign-built textile machinery. During his speech before a substantial audience, including representatives from the Board of Trade, he took the opportunity to question the Government's current policy on duty free importation of textiles from the Commonwealth.

> Ever since I was a boy I have been connected in some way with the textile industry, and during the whole of this time there has been constant pressure to contract. I think there are those who will never be satisfied till the industry has been contracted out of existence. I wonder what would have happened to other industries in the country had they been subjected to the sort of competition to which the textile industry has been subjected during the last year (hear, hear and applause). The opening proceedings and speeches were extensively reported in the Guardian, the Financial Times and the US Daily News Record.

During the 1960s import penetration increased by 25% on a base of 41.5%, and both employers and trade unions exerted great pressure on Parliament. From 1965 to 1970 the Labour Party were in Government and in response to criticism Douglas Jay, President of the Board of Trade, in replying to the debate on 20 March 1967, endeavoured to deflect responsibility from duty free imports to the industry's inefficiency!

> If we ignore wages and comparative wage levels altogether, and consider yarn production per spindle as measured by kg per year, the figure for 1964, the latest for which we have GATT figures, was 43.5 in the United Kingdom, compared with 53 in Italy, 63 in France, 65 in Japan, 71 in Belgium, 68 in Australia and 86 in Portugal – so it is not just a question of wage levels in Portugal, and 126 in the United States. If we consider cloth production per loom the comparison is rather more favourable to the United Kingdom. The figure was 2100 here, which is better than Portugal and Japan, but worse than France and Australia, and slightly less than half that of Belgium and the United States.

These figures, although most probably correct, are not the slightest use as an indication of either labour productivity or machine output per unit. Productivity is a measure of the ratio between hours of operator activity and an intellectually respectable index of performance or achievement such as in spinning (OHP) operator hours per specified output units, e.g. 100kg, with an indication of the yarn linear density, or in weaving (OHPPM) operative hours per million pick metres. The explanation of the absurdity of considering the GATT figures as indicative of productivity or production is that a spinning spindle can produce between 2 and 100 grams per hour depending on yarn linear density, and a loom can produce between 2 and 25 metres of fabric per hour depending on pick density. Also shift patterns in some countries are government controlled and annual hours of operation vary from about 2500 to 6800 per year. It would be unreasonable to expect Government officials to understand the minutiae of textile manufacturing, but one would expect at least the application of common sense. Even the Minister should have realised that these figures were nonsense. If the UK was more efficient than Japan, but less than half as efficient as Belgium, it does not require MENSA intelligence to conclude that Belgium must be between two and three times as efficient as Japan! Two of our spinning mills in Ashton's, one of which had been completely re-equipped, had 'productivity figures' on the Minister's index of 127 and 134, that is higher than the figure for US mills. Although these were well equipped and efficiently operated units, the figures do not justify, nor do I believe, that we had reached parity with US mills.

I decided to respond to the Jay contribution to Government thinking and addressed a letter for inclusion in the correspondence section of the *Guardian* to set the record straight.[9] To my surprise it was elevated to a feature article of thirteen column-inches under the title 'Lancashire and the Efficiency Myth'. I had included a table from a German source 'Die Textil-Industrie in Europe und der Welt' which showed the rates of change of the production of twenty textile producing countries, both developed and developing, between 1950 and 1965 in five year intervals. This showed that the UK industry compared well with most other industries, which was particularly creditable as the re-equipment phase of the 1959 Cotton Industry Act was wrecked in 1962 by the premature and progressive increase in market penetration of duty-free textiles from low-wage economies, culminating in 1966 in that masterly negotiation when 10% was added to quotas to make an open-ended global quota negotiable. Dr W. T. Kroese, managing director of Nyverdal-Ten-Cate, the largest horizontal textile group in Holland, wrote in his annual report in 1965:

> In the Netherlands we can consider ourselves fortunate that in a letter dated 15th November 1964 addressed to the Permanent Economic Affairs Committee of the Lower House, the Minister for Economic Affairs stood up for the industry. One of the statements made was that it was not the intention of the government to sacrifice the cotton and rayon industry along the lines of what happened on the other side of the channel for political Commonwealth reasons.

Dr F. Richter, writing in the German 'Spinner, Weber and Textilveredlung' for March, stated in his article dealing with the German textile industry's views on Britain and the Common Market:

> The question of the Commonwealth was far from being resolved in the 1962–63 discussions, even though both sides were able to point to outline formulations on 3rd August 1963, of future trade agreements with India, Ceylon, Pakistan and Hong Kong. At the time the problem was to reconcile the Common Markets cautious import policy from low cost countries with the British policy which blindly sacrificed its own industry in favour of Commonwealth interests.

Dr Adenauer, the German Federal Chancellor in a speech in the Bundestag on the 11 October 1962, indicated that the danger to the German textile industry of low-cost imports was recognised. If Mr Jay and his advisers were unaware where the responsibility resided, they knew in Holland and Germany.

The Cotton Spinners and Manufacturers Association circulated the *Guardian* article to all MPs representing textile constituencies. It generated considerable flack and was widely quoted, but the rate of increase of market penetration never fell, but continued linearly with time.

VII. Some Internal Problems

As outlined in previous sections, the reason for the UK as a major industrial nation uniquely no longer possessing a textile industry is due entirely to government's progressive handing-over 90% of the market to Commonwealth NDCs. The industry predicted the outcome in every negotiation with Government, or its surrogate the Cotton Board, from 1952 until there were less workers involved in spinning and weaving than in Mauritius. The plurality of trade union organisations complicated transition from one technology to another, and trade union negotiation involved management in several days of negotiation per month, which should have been available to deal with manufacturing problems and developments. In Ashton's one complex manufacturing yarn and fabric and making up bed linen and towels we negotiated with ten unions. In many companies this was an impediment to transition to verticality. Even the Textile and Clothing Strategy Group had three trade union members in a total of ten.

The industry also had a much greater spread of technical and commercial competence than other European industries, which reduced the industry's statistical indices of productivity and efficiency. The top 20% was in a different league to the bottom 40%, and invariably compared favourably with the best in Europe. To some extent this was the result of the two cartels, the Yarn Spinners Association and the Finishers Association, pitched at a level to provide a survival selling price for the least efficient, which imposed great price pressure on the weavers, sandwiched between fixed yarn prices and fixed bleaching, printing and finishing prices. This was demonstrated by the comparative rates of mill closures in the 1950s and 1960s, and the relatively small penetration of automatic looms and shuttle-less weaving machines in horizontal weaving organisations. Both the cartels and the retention of obsolete weaving machinery in horizontally organised mills were indirectly the result of the duty-free imports as horizontal weaving margins were subliminal to non-existent. The detachment of marketing from manufacturing in the great majority of organisations was another major organisational defect. All the American mills in Table 3 were verticalised up to the final transaction with the customer. This avoided the trading situation in which it was impossible to operate a capital-intensive industry.[10]

> During this period, retailers sales declined by 10%, but they reduced their stocks by 25%, passing on still lower orders down the chain through the wholesalers and garment manufacturers until the converters sales of cotton goods had their worst decline of 44%. Converters likewise shortened their commitments, reducing their purchases from weavers by 60%, until finally spinners sales fell by 70%.

The dislocation during periods of difficult trading was not the only deleterious effect of the UK supply chain, in which cotton brokers, yarn agents, converters and merchants added to cost without material change to the value of the product.

The industry's manufacturing costs were largely determined by the industry's equipment that, in the period under review, in most mills never reached the standard of either our European or American competitors. Several of the European industries were completely renewed after war destruction either by American or government assistance. The German industry was virtually re-established with the latest machinery in new buildings, and the American industry, which was modern at the onset of a relatively short war, emerged relatively unscathed. The UK industry was carrying a high proportion of obsolete equipment due to the diminution of the formerly enormous export trade between 1925 and 1939. In 1945 the industry was required to re-activate cocooned machinery and turn its most productive equipment over to multi-shift working with no financial assistance from government, with the exception of the re-equipment subsidy provided for the spinning section. From 1952 onwards imports from Commonwealth NDCs depressed margins disproportionate to their initial volume, but as quotas continued to increase, confidence in the prospect of obtaining a return on investment in fixed assets was severely undermined. Sections 2 and 4 review the government's subliminal assistance to the textile manufacturing industry from 1948 up to 2000. Even after scrapping 57.8% of the spindles and 42.6% of the looms under the 1959 Cotton Industry Act, 26% of the spindles that remained were either obsolete or obsolescent and 66% of the looms were obsolete. In 1962, coincident with implementation of the Act, imports predominantly duty-free were above 40% and moving inexorably towards half the available market. Simultaneously, textile machinery was rapidly increasing in both sophistication and cost.

It appears to have escaped the attention of the DTI and the Textile Clothing Strategy Group that textile manufacturing is now in the upper decile of capital intensity, bracketed with petroleum products manufacture, and the reference to 'traditional', 'mature' and 'smokestack' industry is at least forty years out of date. In 1955 looms increased in cost from £450 to £3000, increasing over time until 1995, reaching £75,000 for the multi-phase weaving machine. The cost per rotor for open-end spinning machine escalated similarly since introduction at 40,000 rpm and now running at 150,000 rpm. In a feasibility study for a 'Phoenix' mill to re-activate the industry, the project cost for 13 open-end spinning machines and 48 multi-phase weaving machine installation in new buildings was £22,882,000, or £16,247,900 in suitably modified existing buildings, or respectively £177,000 or £125,900 per worker inclusive of administration. This massive transition in capital intensity was well established during the period of wafer-thin margins, and contraction of facilities and growth in duty-free imports shown in Figure 1. None of these internal problems confronted our competitors in Europe and the USA, where imports were being restricted by adequate tariff protection, contemporary with a wide variety of grants and concessions. Our competitors were receiving very different treatment from their governments.[11]

> After years of being neglected in Washington, the American textile producers have in the past twelve months become the most courted industrial group in the nation.
>
> New depreciation allowances have been granted, assistance is offered in R & D, international restrictions on imports have been negotiated, and the tariff commission are seriously considering making the industry's competitors pay in the form of an imports levy for the export subsidy enjoyed by the American cotton growers, all this it seems, stems from the 'astronomical' rise in imports from 2% to 6% of the market, figures that may raise a wry smile in Lancashire.

The last paragraph of section 6 includes opinions of some of the leading European politicians and textile manufacturers. All our competitors were fully aware of 'the situation on the other side of the channel', and unequivocally identified those responsible for it.

VIII. An Alternative to Atrophy

Three years have now elapsed since the Textile and Clothing Strategy Group set out to prevent the two industries reaching 'a critical mass' situation. This was an unrealistic objective from the outset as the textile manufacturing industry had reached this situation about 1985, and currently (2003) has no short staple cotton and man-made fibre spinning sector, a weaving sector down to 6000 productive looms and weaving machines (Sulzer Survey), and a finishing sector in an advanced state of decline as its major remaining activity, the beneficiation of imported duty-free loom-state fabric, is replaced by imported garments. There is no evidence of reversal of the 2000 trend in either employment or production. It was demonstrated in section 5 that a ten-month analysis of mill closures in one textile journal indicated a rate of contraction similar to the two-year contraction from 1998 to 2000, prior to the TCSG assuming responsibility for reversing the 8000 redundancies per year from textile manufacturing organisations (source: Office for National Statistics Annual Business Inquiry). No comparative figures of any of the benchmark figures provided in the report 'National Strategy for the Textile and Clothing Industry' were included in the 2003 progress report 'Making it Happen'. All the evidence available indicates an increase in imports, a reduction in added value, and a reduction in capacity in all three sectors of textile manufacturing and in the clothing industry. The 55 recommendations that aggregate the TCSG strategy have clearly not achieved the declared objective, and an alternative to atrophy is essential if the detritus of the textile industry and the rapidly declining clothing industry are not to perish without trace.

The only clothing activities surviving in western economies are either in the formation of horizontal linkages with textile manufacturing in 'fibre to garment' organisations, or as independent quick response manufacturers (QRM), which necessitates a very high standard of efficiency minimising the cost differences between domestic and NDC production. Warburton and Warner discussed the conditions necessary for an effective QRM activity in a western economy in reference (5). As loom-state fabric will no longer be provided for the clothing industry, and as it is now possible to produce profitably in the UK and sell at NDC landed selling prices, horizontal association as practised by many organisations in the USA and Italy is now possible. The essential requirement is comparable garment manufacturing costs to US costs in linked or QRM organisations. From the evidence available it should have been apparent to the TCSG that the only hope for a survival of a significant part of the clothing industry was for fabric to be provided from domestic mills, at economic prices which could be converted in well-organised and equipped clothing plants so as to be able to compete effectively with imported garments. Benetton do it in Italy and Kellwood Corporation, a $2 billion Fortune 500 Company, do it in the USA.

Of the 55 recommendations only four relate to textile manufacturing, and none of these relate to recommendations for either organisational change or capital investment. As capital investment as a general topic was discussed in 134 works in a 48-page report, the textile machinery revolution and its impact on loom-state manufacturing costs was apparently either not considered relevant or within the capacity of the working party to investigate. This is surprising as it was fully appreciated even outside the textile manufacturing fraternity.[12]

> Perversely, technical advances in spinning and weaving now make the logic of cheap labour in this part of the supply chain less compelling.

A consultant in supply chain economics was better informed than the organisation selected to investigate two industries and recommend a strategy to re-activate textile manufacturing and avoid the imminent elimination of the clothing industry and the horizontal finishing sector, as apparel imports progressively replaced loom-state fabric.

Had a comprehensive investigation been made such as the 300-page Textile Council 'Cotton and Allied Textiles' Volumes 1 and 2, important and relevant conclusions would have been the outcome, similar to those considered in the penultimate sentence of paragraph 3 of section 4.

For example, what was the ratio between textile workers and garment workers after application of 2000 technology in both activities? In 'Phoenix' mill, considered later, 129 workers inclusive of administration, produce 893,000m^2 per week of a high quality combed cotton and polyester blend print-base fabric, an output of 6922m^2 per textile worker. If this were to be made into dresses with say 2.25m^2 per dress including waste, it would make 396,890 garments. If the garments per worker per week = 100 and there is a 25% non-productive staffing.

$$\text{Number of garment workers} = \frac{\text{Woven production}\left(\text{m}^2\right)\times(1+\text{overhead ratio})}{\left(\text{m}^2/\text{garment. inc waste}\right)\times\left(\text{machinist weekly shift production}\right)}$$

$$\text{Number of garment workers} = \frac{893{,}000\times(1+0.25)}{2.25\times100} = 4961$$

$$\text{Ratio garment workers to textile workers} = 4961/129 = 38.5$$

Obviously this will vary with different values of weekly machinist production, fabric m^2/garment and non-productive labour ratio, but for a variety of combinations examined the ratio varies between 25 and 40, i.e. 1000 textile workers supporting between 25,000 and 40,000 garment workers, with most of the examples between 25,000 and 30,000. This extraordinary result is the consequence of the enormous transfer of labour input from the workers to the machines. For example, a weaver would have a minimum of eight machines of M8300, or six weavers for the 48 machine installation producing the 893,000m^2 per week, or 24 on all shifts; a weekly production per weaver of 37,200m^2. A similar situation arises with one spinner supervising four open-end rotor-spinning machines each of 280 rotors and producing 9200kg of yarn per week. The preparation processes and weaving preparation are equally productive.

The same rigorous approach is essential to design a Phoenix garment operation capable of achieving the QRM level of costs both to operate independently and also integrated with a Phoenix spinning and weaving operation.

After proving one manufacturing activity and one garment operation, three other single product mills could be designed for denim, poplin shirting and bed 'linen'. As the last two products cannot be produced on multi-phase weaving machines, the bed sheeting for width and the poplin shirting for warp-end density, both would be manufactured on Tsudakoma ZAX single phase air-jet machines capable of commercial speeds of 2600 m/min weft insertion rate. Phase 1 to prove the production cost and quality standard could be produced for £23 million in new buildings. Phase 2 which has not been investigated to feasibility study standard, is unlikely to cost more than £84 million, and to produce less than 135 million m^2 per annum, or 177 million m^2 for the four mills at a cost of approximately £107 million. The industry has already received £90 million to little apparent effect.

The Phoenix mill producing 893,000m^2 per week will provide fabric for between 3000 and 4000 workers, depending on the fabric and the garment time rating, and the productive labour ratio.

For a wide range of fabrics, products, and garment organisations, one textile worker will provide sufficient fabric to maintain between 20 and 30 garment workers. The 129 workers in Phoenix will be capable of supporting 3000 garment workers. The Phase 1 plus Phase 2 production would maintain about 14,000 garment workers in employment, and would make a significant reduction in the massive import bill which moves inexorably from the £15.4 billion between 2000 to a realistic prediction of £16.9 billion in 2003, and inevitably rising to £21.8 billion unless UK production is reactivated with a Twenty-first Century Strategy.

IX. Financing Possibilities

The major textile manufacturers with the necessary capital resources have moved their manufacturing activities overseas, taking the added value of spinning and weaving, and more recently finishing and garment manufacturing into low wage economies. They no longer provide a financing possibility. In Germany and Japan the investment banks provide this function, whereas the UK banks have shown little desire to invest in UK industry in general and textile manufacturing in particular. Inward investment is highly favoured by government, but the unique trading environment in which the UK textile industry has been obliged to operate is well publicised overseas, and this source can be eliminated as a possibility. The American industry has had massive support from government from 1962 onwards and this is ongoing, but the phantom £90 million is unlikely to be extended unless positive evidence of post-2005 viability is forthcoming.

Many new mills in the NDCs are financed in the following way. A common formula is 51% equity and 49% loan capital, the latter supplied by organisations such as the Industrial Finance Corporation (IFC), the European Development Bank (EDB), the African Development Bank (ADB), and our own Commonwealth Development Corporation (CDC). In most cases two or three of these development banks contribute the 49% in equal proportions. In some cases, particularly if the project is a new company as well as a new project, the lenders agree to a 'grace period' of two or three years during which repayment is not required. The equity is usually subscribed by an industrialist with an established interest, or an entrepreneur with an interest in a potentially profitable investment. In most cases, particularly if the project is a large one, government will invest through a para-statal such as the country's Development Corporation. The equity could be provided 40% by the industrialist and 11% by the government para-statal. When the loans are discharged in, say, ten years, the investor will hold 78.4% of the equity and the government 21.6%. If the investor invested 51%, he would have an operation worth £22.88 million (if it was Phoenix) for which he invested £11.67 million and having had ten years interest on his investment. If he only subscribed 40%, he would still have control of the business worth £22.88 million, having invested £9.15 million and received interest for the previous ten years.

The European Union may be prepared to support the Phase 1 investment for two reasons. The massive duty-free imports from NDCs that have penetrated the UK market above 90% and still increasing have substantially relieved pressure on the other European textile manufacturers.

Also it would be logical to site the mills in the four areas of unrest in Lancashire, all of which are traditional run-down textile communities. This would obviously be conditional on the UK government taking an equal share. The European textile manufacturers will also prefer to compete with UK production than beneficiated duty-free loom-state fabric.

It may take a few years, but repatriation of the UK companies which emigrated to take advantage of the low labour costs could well find it uneconomical to remain. Three influences will contribute. The textile machinery revolution is no use for the mills in NDCs; if 20% is added to current financial costs (depreciation + interest) to achieve a 50% labour cost reduction – an almost impossible combination; the mills in India, South Korea and Indonesia increase costs by an average of 5.8 cents per metre (7.0%).[13] Even 1995 technology costs too much for the lowest total cost situations. The situation is complicated by high interest costs of 18% and over. Secondly hourly wages are increasing massively in some NDCs. Labour costs in South Korea have increased by 300% between 1991 and 2002, the associated labour costs increasing from 6% to 12% of total fabric costs, and similar increases discussed in section 5, are bringing some NDCs up to the lowest costs in Europe. The textile machinery revolution has a dual affect. Not only does it make it possible to manufacture at UK labour rates at lower costs than NDCs, but the spinning and weaving machinery also produces yarn and fabric that is technically and aesthetically superior. This type of machinery significantly increases costs, and retaining an overseas location in NDCs precludes producing the highest quality merchandise. This repatriation may not be early enough to provide immediate funds for a Phoenix operation, as the success of such an operation is essential to stimulate repatriation.

X. The Nation and the Consumer

The Nation is vitally affected in maintaining GDP at a healthy level and avoiding balance of payment problems with textile imports at £15.41 million in 2000; with the probability of the remaining £6.46 billion of added value disappearing at the estimated current rate, the import value could be £22 billion by 2007. The National Security situation must be considered unsatisfactory.

The USA have 300 ‘combat sensitive’ textiles, none of which are permitted to be purchased outside the USA, and other European countries have similar classified restrictions. Is it sustainable to have defence ordnance manufactured 3000 miles away with no facilities for domestic production? Even if delivery in wartime could be guaranteed, which is unlikely, are we content to have ballistic or fireproof garments manufactured overseas? The run-down of the textile areas and the reduction of living standards by textile workers formerly earning good industrial wages being re-employed on activities paying minimum wages, has produced the civil disturbances and National Front penetration. It would be politically and economically desirable to make these areas the locations for the new high-tech textile industry.

The textile consumers in the UK have been subjected to an enormous government sponsored cock-up. The admission of fabric from

Commonwealth NDCs provided the clothing industry with fabric at least 20% cheaper than that available to the competition, providing the manufacturers with the opportunity to supply the UK customer with the lowest cost garments in the western economy, at the cost to the country of massively reduced GDP and taxation revenue. The actual outcome was the highest apparel costs in the west, considerably higher than garments manufactured in US mills. In 2000, for example, Cone Mills denim slacks were sold in Walmart stores at the dollar equivalent of £22 when the identical article was sold in the UK at prices varying from £30 to £40, and poplin shirts at the equivalent of £11 when the UK equivalent quality was selling at £16. Similarly, sheet sets manufactured by Springs, and towels by Cannon were comparably lower in cost than the UK articles. Textile prices in France and Belgium were also appreciably cheaper. The 20% loom state advantage had been more than offset by inefficiency in conversion and presumably increased margins. The retailers, led by Marks and Spencer, finally realised that the existing supply chain was uneconomical and declared their intention to purchase overseas from the source of the loom state fabric. Now the country is gradually losing the finishing and garment manufacturing added value (£6.46 billion in 2000). Inevitably, the £15.41 billion of imports in 2000 will increase up to the 2000 turnover value of £21.94 billion as contraction of textile finishing and garment manufacture continues.

Section 2 through section 6 outlined government's participation in the textile industry's affairs under two administrations covering a period of 55 years; during which time I had the opportunity to work in association with several governments in both western and newly industrialised countries for some 20 years. They contrast with the years from 1946 to 1970, during which I worked with one of Britain's largest textile manufacturers, and Britain's largest textile chemical fibre to garment manufacturer.

The following quotation from Lewis Ord's 'Industrial Facts and Fallacies' clearly identifies the reasons for UK's indifferent industrial performance for the major part of the century.

> American industrialists are not entitled to the whole of the praise for better performance, nor the British industrialist for the whole of the blame for the backwardness of British Industry to-day. The wiser industrial policies adopted by American governments are the real foundation of the American lead. British politicians must shoulder most of the blame for British industry being so far behind … the industrial policies of governments, the things they do and refuse to do – these are the things that control the efficiency of industry.

This opinion is consistent with my own industrial experience of 26 years in the UK, 20 years in industry overseas, and 10 years in partial retirement as an observer of the UK industrial scene in the last decade of the twentieth century and the early years of the twenty-first. This observation and related correspondence with government departments has not identified any change in government ex-cathedra decisions in areas in which their knowledge is frequently historical or incorrect. That this opinion is either unrepresentative, historical, or peculiar to experience in one industry, can be easily disposed of because Lord Kings Norton (Harold Roxbee Cox), the distinguished aeronautical engineer, clearly had similar experiences in another industry and at a loftier level.

The following extract is from his obituary.[14]

> This (government participation in jet propulsion) perhaps, ignited his life long concern that British Governments seem especially ill equipped to provide a sympathetic environment for technological advance. Apart from the scientific branch of the Civil Service, which is 'always on tap but never on top', there are very few scientists and no engineers in government. 'Certainly our government never seems to know how to handle new technology and nurture innovation in our most important national industries' he argued.

Similar and somewhat more immoderate opinions have appeared regularly in the editorial and correspondence sections of the professional engineering journals. One correspondent to 'Manufacturing Engineer', one of the journals of The Institution of Electrical Engineers, claimed that the BOT and DTI had collectively squandered without account \$(⅓) trillions in the previous 50 years. He did not specify if this was an American or European trillion (10^{12} or 10^{18}), and neither did he provide the source of this unlikely information. Even if we assume that the 10^{12} trillion was intended, this corresponds to £132,800,000 per week! Aggregate expenditure from the Delorean wonder car to the Siemens chip plant, with numerous automotive disasters between, all apparently without public accounting for each project. Investment in a textile industry re-establishment project must by comparison be small change. What would be a reasonable investment in a strategy the object of which was to kick-start a Twenty-first Century Textile Industry capable of trading profitably in a post-2005 trading environment without any tariff protection? In Europe and the USA, 2000 technology is already producing predictable results, and interest in tariff protection and 'level playing fields' (the TCSG fixation) is no longer influencing capital investment projects in progressive companies.

Almost 50 years ago Harold Wilson, then shadow President of the Board of Trade (1954), produced the policy document 'Plan for Cotton'. Duty-free importation of yarn and fabric had already made significant market penetration (20%), and the trade unions in the industry were highly critical of the outcome of the 1948 Re-equipment Subsidy and made a unilateral approach to Harold Wilson. The 'Plan for Cotton' was the only sound plan ever to emerge from government during the second half of the twentieth century. The fourteen recommendations clearly demonstrated that not only had the real problems of the industry been correctly identified, but that innovations and sound technically based solutions had been advanced for their solution. At last the nettle of vertical organisation was to be grasped, the Yarn Spinners Association selling price arrangements were to be continuously monitored by the Board, stabilization of the home market by using government purchases as a stabilizing factor, and by a new type of utility scheme based on long runs of government guaranteed orders to standard specifications, re-equipment to be expedited by tax incentives with State provision for buildings (with one or more pilot factories to show how), and the raw cotton commission to be re-constituted. There was clearly a professional involvement in the Plan that had not been introduced in Whitehall. Unfortunately, Harold Wilson remained on the opposition benches for eleven more years, and by 1965 imports had reached 55%, and were increasing at a steady linear rate. With market penetration increased by 275%, the problems had massively changed and required even more radical solution, which was not forthcoming.

The Board of Trade response to this situation was to endeavour to deflect attention from the indefensible 50% duty-free import situation by claiming that the UK industry was incapable of competing effectively even with European and American competition, in economies paying even larger wages. Although this manoeuvre was discredited in both the national and trade press, as Figure 1 shows the rate of penetration continued at an annual steady rate of 3% of the total available 1950 market until 1970. The subsequent reduction in rate of penetration, which averaged only 22% of the rate between 1952 and 1970, was not the result of any government quota restriction, but to the increasing financial and administration difficulty of procuring speciality business, and of dealing with greater resistance to capitulation. However, since 2000 the rate of contraction appears to be very similar to that shown in official statistics for 1998–2000, i.e. 17% per annum.

XI. Epilogue

The title of this review states that the years between 1945 and 2000 were the industry's terminal years. As shown in Figure 1 the period started with 425,000 spindles, 340,000 looms, and 220,000 employees. The number of employees then increased to 320,000 by 1959 in response to government's exhortation. The comparative figures at the close of 2000 were a non-existent short staple spinning sector, 6000 looms and 40,000 employees. Furthermore, the labour force had contracted from 56,000 in 1998 to 40,000 in 2000, showing no signs of even a reduction in the rate of factory closures and redundancies of 8000 per year. When the Textile and Clothing Strategy Group released this report in 2000 the textile manufacturing industry consisted of some 6000 looms and weaving machines dependent 100% on duty-free imported yarn, a finishing sector based on finishing imported loom state fabric from the NDCs, a source of supply already declining rapidly as the garment importation policy was implemented. The clothing sector's future was equally precarious. The terms of reference were unrelated to the industry's lamentable condition that was fifteen years beyond its 'critical mass', which the new strategy was to prevent. Not only was it no longer an industry, a situation recognised by industrialists and textile machinery manufacturers in overseas countries, but it was for the first time in a hundred years facing a situation in which all equipment installed pre-1995 was obsolescent and all equipment installed pre-1990 obsolete. This situation has been outlined in sections 7 and 8.

As discussed in section 8, An Alternative to Atrophy, the textile manufacturing industry is currently in the upper decile of capital intensity bracketed with petroleum products, and clothing manufacture is in the lowest decile bracketed with furniture and leather goods. It would appear indefensible to contrive a situation in which an industry in the upper decile of capital intensity should be allowed to disappear at the expense of retaining an industry in the lowest decile.

Ricardo's Theory of Competitive Advantage turned on its head! The only clothing industry still retained in western economies is where the country operates an efficient and profitable textile industry. USA, Italy and Switzerland are typical examples, and the only hope of retaining a clothing industry in a high wage economy is either as an efficient integrated unit in a horizontally structured organisation, or as a highly efficient independent specialist QRM operation.

The £15 million provided to re-establish a viable textile manufacturing industry, saving the potential survivors, was derisory. Table 6 shows the capital intensity of the basic machines in a spinning and

Table 6 Typical Capital Intensity of Textile Machinery and Related Modern Allocations

	Machine Cost (£)	*Machines per Employee*
Multi-phase weaving machine	130,000	12
OE Spinning machines 280 position	480,000	3
Carding machine	80,000	20
Combing machine	105,000	12
Sizing machine	500,000	0.5

Note: including proportionate ancillaries.

Cost per Hour of One Workplace

Capital Cost Per workplace (£)	*Annual charge %*	*Cost of one workplace/hour for a range of operating hours* 5000	7000	8760
100,000	15	3.0	2.1	1.7
	25	5.0	3.6	2.9
	35	7.0	5.0	4.0
500,000	15	15.0	10.7	8.6
	25	25.0	17.8	14.2
	35	35.0	25.0	20.0
1,000,000	15	30.0	21.5	17.2
	25	50.0	35.7	28.6
	35	70.0	50.0	40.0
1,500,000	15	45.0	32.1	25.8
	25	75.0	53.4	42.9
	35	105.0	75.0	60.0
2,000,000	15	60.0	42.9	34.3
	25	100.0	71.4	57.1
	35	140.0	100.0	79.9

Note: International mill operating hours vary from 4429 in Poland to 8760 in Zambia.

weaving operation with 2000 technology. It will be seen that one workplace (one worker's assignment on the equipment) varies from £0.25 million to £1.6 million, with an average of £1,465,000 with the exclusion of the sizing machine. There are, of course, four shift workers for each assignment and some ancillary workers, technicians and mechanics, but in a new mill £180,000 per worker in the plant is average, inclusive of buildings and plant. Phoenix 1 averages £177,380 per worker. It is also obvious that continuous four-shift operation is necessary to make this equipment economical. It also follows that an employee working a four-shift system at £8 per hour with a workplace cost of £1.5 million in an organisation with a (depreciation plus interest) charge of 20%, would have a workplace/hour cost of £34.3 per hour. Such organisations as Lauffenmuhle in Germany and Ramtex in the USA are fully committed to air jet spinning and multi-phase weaving and have no worries about competition in 2005 when the WTO dispensation becomes a requirement, or with the angle of the NDCs playing field.

£23 million would have financed Phoenix 1 and established the viability of competitive and profitable textile manufacturing in the UK, both currently and post the 2005 WTO dispensation. This has already been established in three western countries. The £95 million already expended by the DTI would have built the four Phoenix mills, providing work for at least 12,000 garment workers in efficient plants and providing between 150 and 200 million m^2 of dress fabric, denim and work-wear, sheeting, and poplin shirting, the actual annual production construction-dependent. This would make a significant addition to GDP and reduction of the textile import figure currently moving up from the £15.41 billion in 2000 to the £21.94 billion turnover. This is inevitable unless the TCSG strategy of reinforcing obsolete technology in dozens of different initiatives is replaced by a Phoenix programme, capitalising on the textile machinery revolution.

Notes

1. Bowker, B., *Seven Terrible Years (1920–1927)*; Leonard and Virginia Woolf *Under the Hammer (1921)*; Daniel, G. W. *The Early English Cotton Trade*, University Press, Manchester 1920; Robson, R. *The Cotton Industry in Britain*, Macmillan, London (1957).
2. Streat, E. R. S., *Lancashire and Whitehall: The Diary of Sir Raymond Streat*, vol. 2 (1939–57), Manchester University Press, pp. 337–40.
3. Ormerod, A., 'The Prospects of the British Cotton Industry', *Textile Recorder*, December 1962, February, March and April 1963.
4. Streat, E. R. S., *Lancashire and Whitehall*, Epilogue, p. 937.
5. Warburton, R. D. H., *Domestic Apparel Manufacturing. When is it Competitive?*, 2000, National Textile Centre, USA; Warburton, R. D. H. and Warner, S.B., *How much quick response manufacturing can a business afford?*, University of Massachusetts, USA.
6. International Textile Manufacturers Federation, Zurich, Switzerland, International Production Cost Comparisons (Spinning and Weaving) 1991, 1994, 1997 and 2001.
7. Ormerod, A., *An Industrial Odyssey*, The Textile Institute, Manchester, 1996, pp. 117–27.

8. Ormerod, A., *An Industrial Odyssey*, pp. 158–61, 170–3.
9. Ormerod, A., *An Industrial Odyssey*, pp. 185–90.
10. Robson, R., *The Cotton Industry in Britain*, Macmillan (1957), p. 175.
11. *The Financial Times*, April 1962.
12. Hamilton, P., 'Bankrolling the Global Supply Chain', Textile Institute World Conference Proceedings 2000.
13. Ormerod, A., 'The Viability of the Textile Manufacturing in Developed Economies in the New Millennium', *The Journal of the Textile Institute*, 91 (2000), pp. 197–9.
14. Tucker, A., 'The Obituary of Lord Kings Norton', *The Guardian*, 23 December 1997.

Index